CROSSWORD PUZZLES

This book belongs to:

CROSSWORD

A crossword is a word puzzle and word search game. The game's goal is to fill the squares with letters, forming words or phrases, by solving clues, which lead to the answers. The crossword puzzle game certainly is the best way to enhance your IQ and keeps your mind active. Crossword puzzles are well-known brain games. They are the finest ways of relaxation and rejuvenation.

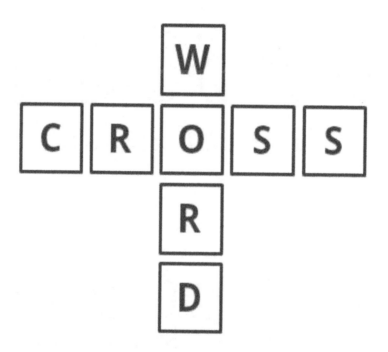

One puzzle per page Very easy to read

All puzzles have solutions

Puzzle #1

Across
1. Dissolves materials
2. Loved very much
3. Ordinary
4. Respecting God
5. Without a home
6. Boring
7. Beautiful, powerful, or causing great admiration and respect
8. Very respected
9. Unhappy or sorry
10. Not in danger or likely to be harmed

Down
11. Extremely ugly or bad
12. On or onto a ship, aircraft, bus, or train
13. Man
14. Unkind, cruel
15. Careful not to attract too much attention
16. Coming before all others
17. Very well
18. Dark and dirty or difficult to see through
19. Not having something
20. Said or thought by some people to be the stated bad or illegal thing, although you have no proof
21. Refusing to obey
22. Extremely large
23. No water or other liquid in

Puzzle #2

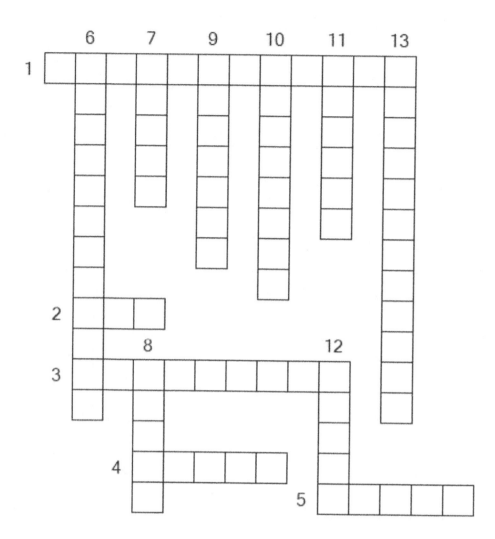

Across
1. Not certain, or wrong in some way
2. Unhappy or sorry
3. Having a lot of energy
4. Easy to understand
5. Containing, tasting of, or similar to nuts

Down
6. Not excited
7. Hard or firm
8. Develop
9. Extremely large
10. Not clear and having no form
11. Damaged
12. Not dirty
13. Feeling of energetic interest

Puzzle #3

Across
1. Not difficult
2. Not dirty
3. Attractive in appearance
4. A foolish idea
5. Careful not to attract too much attention

Down
6. Drinking too much alcohol
7. Unhappy or sorry
8. Shaped like a ball or circle
9. Not wanting others to know
10. Happy or grateful because of something
11. Unacceptable, offensive, violent, or unusual
12. Gradually and secretly causing harm

Puzzle #4

Across
1. Able to stretch
2. Not certain, or wrong in some way
3. Ordinary or usual
4. Unkind, cruel, without sympathy
5. Not wanting others to know
6. Boring

Down
7. Dissolves materials
8. Happy and positive
9. Containing, tasting of, or similar to nuts
10. Unhappy or sorry
11. Fashionable and interesting
12. Worried, nervous
13. Revealing
14. Complicated and difficult to solve

Puzzle #5

Across
1. Extremely surprising, very good, extremely surprised
2. Beautiful, powerful, or causing great admiration and respect
3. Physically attractive
4. Strong and unlikely to break or fail
5. At the same height

Down
6. Extremely large
7. Attractive in appearance
8. The amount of matter in an object
9. Revealing
10. Happy and positive
11. Telling not the true
12. Fact that everyone knows

Puzzle #6

Across
1. No water or other liquid in
2. Fashionable and interesting
3. Not bitter or salty
4. Habit of talking a lot
5. Happening or done quickly and without warning

Down
6. Rightened or worried
7. Disappointed discovering the truth

Puzzle #7

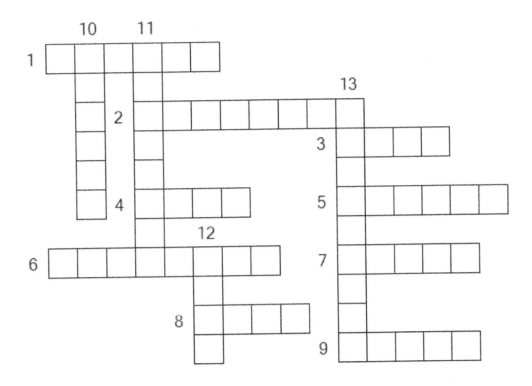

Across
1. Complicated and difficult to solve
2. Glue
3. Not far away in distance
4. Level and smooth
5. Strong and unlikely to break or fail
6. Easily deceived
7. Develop
8. Not in danger or likely to be harmed
9. Not dirty

Down
10. Ordinary or usual
11. Happy or grateful because of something
12. Most excellent, highest quality,
13. Having a lot of energy

Puzzle #8

Across
1. Complicated and difficult to solve
2. Having a pleasant smell
3. Ordinary or usual
4. With clouds
5. Not far away in distance
6. Not bitter or salty
7. Containing, tasting of, or similar to nuts

Down
8. Worried, nervous
9. Attractive or pleasant
10. Extremely surprising, very good, extremely surprised
11. Not guilty of aparticular crime
12. Detestable, repugnant, repulsive, morally very bad

Puzzle #9

Across
1. On or onto a ship, aircraft, bus, or train
2. Without a home
3. No water or other liquid in
4. Fact that everyone knows
5. Not clear and having no form
6. Inside the body

Down
7. Ordinary
8. Man
9. Rounded in a pleasant and attractive way
10. Showing much knowledge
11. Relating to love or a close loving relationship
12. Stupid, unreasonable, silly in a humorous way, things that happen that are unreasonable
13. Having a pleasant smell
14. Loved very much

Puzzle #10

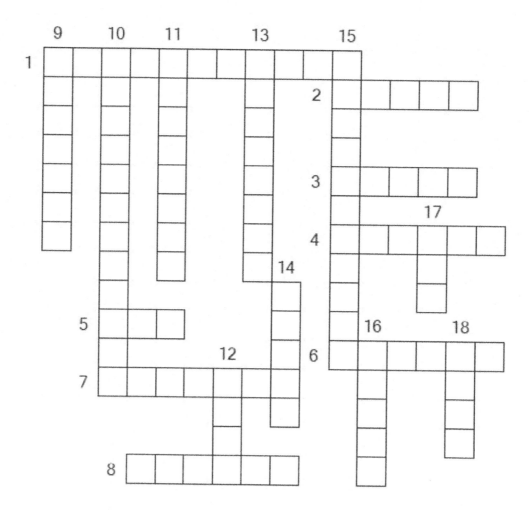

Across
1. Eager to know a lot
2. Coming before all others
3. Causing pain intentionally
4. Rounded in a pleasant and attractive way
5. Unpleasant and causing difficulties or harm, evil, low quality, not acceptable
6. Immediately after the first and before any others
7. Attractive in appearance
8. Happening or done quickly and without warning

Down
9. A foolish idea
10. Not certain, or wrong in some way
11. Not guilty of a particular crime
12. Dissolves materials
13. Happy or grateful because of something
14. Containing, tasting of, or similar to nuts
15. Able to produce the intended result
16. Develop
17. Large in size or amount
18. Not far away in distance

Puzzle #11

Across
1. Boring
2. Not bitter or salty
3. Detestable, repugnant, repulsive, morally very bad
4. Not dirty
5. Officer
6. At the same height
7. Respecting God
8. Loved very much
9. Not far away in distance

Down
10. Not decorated in any way; with nothing added
11. Fashionable and interesting
12. Unpleasant and causing difficulties or harm, evil, low quality, not acceptable
13. Happy and positive
14. Said or thought by some people to be the stated bad or illegal thing, although you have no proof
15. Careful not to attract too much attention

Puzzle #12

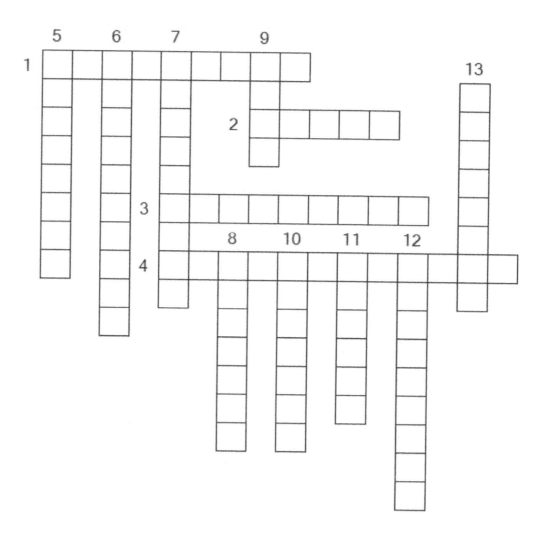

Across
1. Attractive or pleasant
2. Telling not the true
3. Gradually and secretly causing harm
4. Not excited

Down
5. Happy or grateful because of something
6. Unacceptable, offensive, violent, or unusual
7. Extremely funny
8. A foolish idea
9. Man
10. Revealing
11. Strong and unlikely to break or fail
12. Not wanting others to know
13. Careful not to attract too much attention

Puzzle #13

Across
1. Not far away in distance
2. Able to send back light a surface
3. Become pink in the face
4. Attractive or pleasant
5. Ability to do an activity or job well

Down
6. Unhappy because you have nothing to do
7. Not armed
8. Put on one's clothes
9. Extremely ugly or bad
10. Containing, tasting of, or similar to nuts
11. Flesh of a cow
12. Complicated and difficult to solve
13. Unhappy or sorry
14. Man

Puzzle #14

Across
1. Unwilling to give information
2. Complicated and difficult to solve
3. Fashionable and interesting
4. Hard or firm
5. Careful not to attract too much attention
6. Dissolves materials

Down
7. Loved very much
8. Unhappy or sorry
9. Abnormal, deviant, different
10. Officer
11. Avoids risks
12. At the same height
13. Happy and positive
14. No water or other liquid in

Puzzle #15

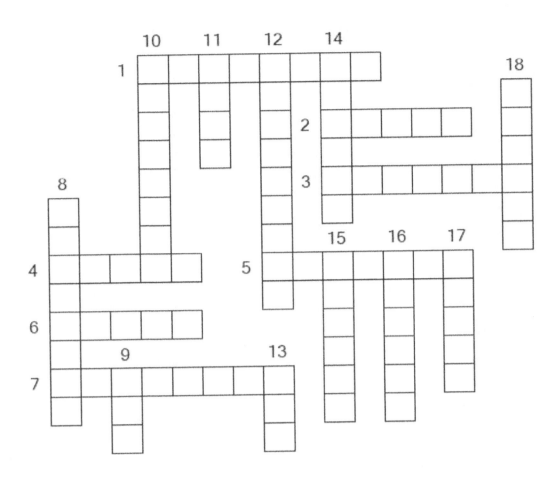

Across
1. Someone who is trying to become successful
2. Shaped like a ball or circle
3. Said or thought by some people to be the stated bad or illegal thing, although you have no proof
4. Containing, tasting of, or similar to nuts
5. Not armed
6. Not dirty
7. Not clear and having no form

Down
8. Not guilty of a particular crime
9. Large in size or amount
10. Abnormal, deviant, different
11. Having less color than usual
12. Morally correct
13. Unhappy or sorry
14. Ordinary or usual
15. On or onto a ship, aircraft, bus, or train
16. Behave like adults
17. Drinking too much alcohol
18. Happening or done quickly and without warning

Puzzle #16

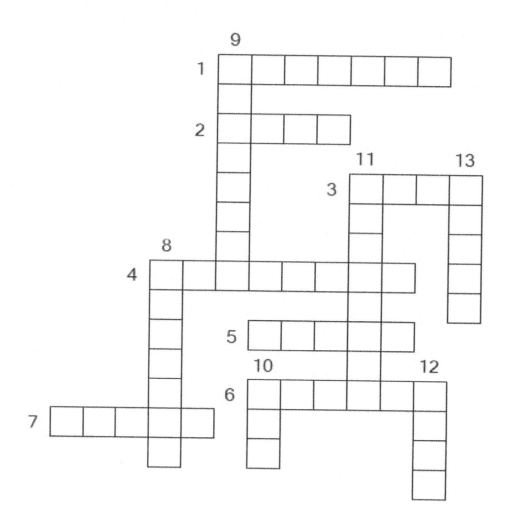

Across
1. Stopping and starting repeatedly
2. Nothing more than
3. Boring
4. Careful not to attract too much attention
5. Containing, tasting of, or similar to nuts
6. Happening or done quickly and without warning
7. Not bitter or salty

Down
8. Harmed or spoiled
9. Without a home
10. Unhappy or sorry
11. Losing against someone
12. Not far away in distance
13. The color of chocolate

Puzzle #17

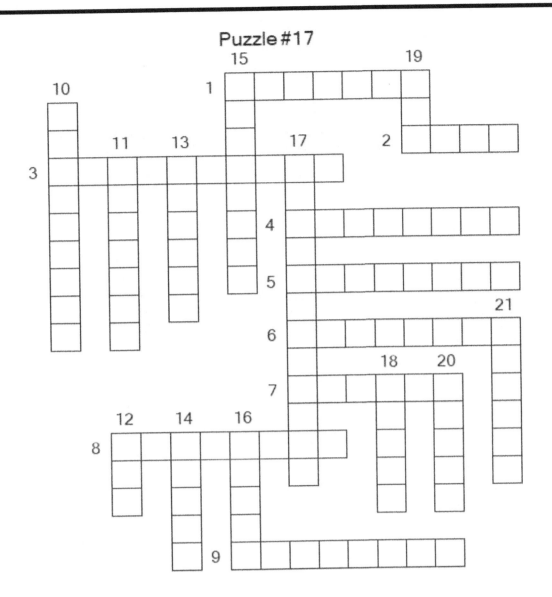

Across
1. Unkind, cruel, without sympathy
2. Boring
3. Unacceptable, offensive, violent, or unusual
4. Inside the body
5. Happy or grateful because of something
6. Relating to love or a close loving relationship
7. Happening or done quickly and without warning
8. Careful not to attract too much attention
9. Losing against someone

Down
10. Attractive or pleasant
11. Revealing
12. No water or other liquid in
13. Poor, unsuccessful, the state of being extremely unhappy
14. Hard or firm
15. Happy and positive
16. Shaped like a ball or circle
17. Not excited
18. Drinking too much alcohol
19. Unhappy or sorry
20. Containing, tasting of, or similar to nuts
21. Fact that everyone knows

Puzzle #18

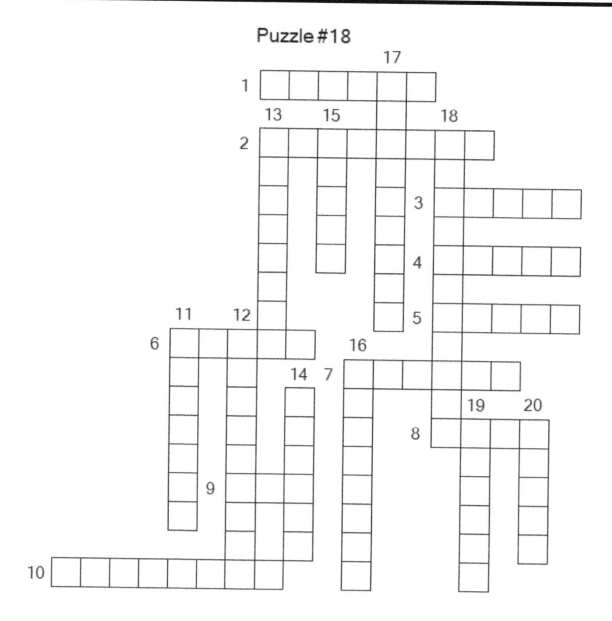

Across
1. Complicated and difficult to solve
2. Very respected
3. Coming before all others
4. Easy to understand
5. Causing pain intentionally
6. Not bitter or salty
7. Fashionable and interesting
8. Not in danger or likely to be harmed
9. Unhappy or sorry
10. Careful not to attract too much attention

Down
11. Unusual and unexpected
12. Limited to only one person
13. Physically attractive
14. Happening or done quickly and without warning
15. Telling not the true
16. Expressing thanks
17. Attractive or pleasant
18. Able to produce the intended result
19. On or onto a ship, aircraft, bus, or train
20. Develop

Puzzle #19

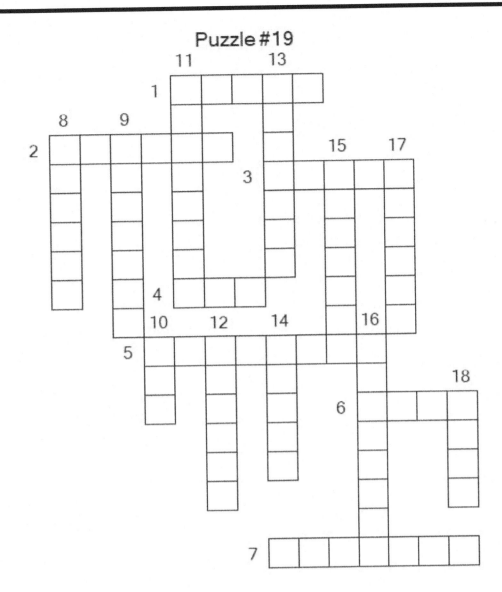

Across
1. Containing, tasting of, or similar to nuts
2. Rounded in a pleasant and attractive way
3. Telling not the true
4. Unhappy or sorry
5. Careful not to attract too much attention
6. Dissolves materials
7. Unkind, cruel, without sympathy

Down
8. Fact that everyone knows
9. Not armed
10. No water or other liquid in
11. Not clear and having no form
12. Happening or done quickly and without warning
13. Revealing
14. Shaped like a ball or circle
15. Extremely large
16. Happy or grateful because of something
17. Fashionable and interesting
18. Boring

Puzzle #20

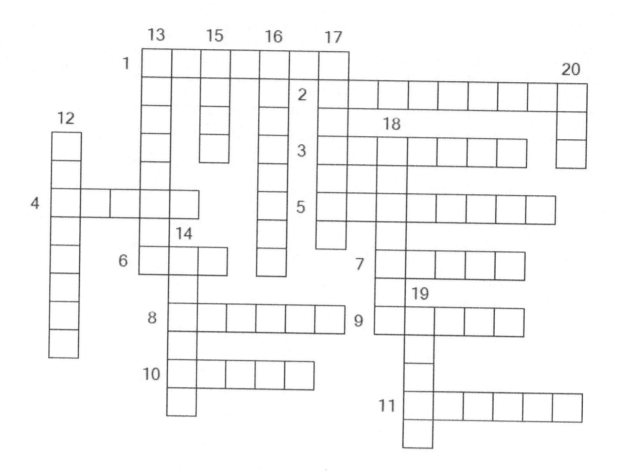

Across

1. Extremely surprising, very good, extremely surprised
2. Morally correct
3. Not armed
4. Containing, tasting of, or similar to nuts
5. Very respected
6. No water or other liquid in
7. Respecting God
8. Clever
9. Drinking too much alcohol
10. Not bitter or salty
11. Ordinary or usual

Down

12. Not guilty of a particular crime
13. Excited, interested, enthusiastic
14. Strong and unlikely to break or fail
15. Dissolves materials
16. Inside the body
17. Complain in an angry way
18. Said or thought by some people to be the stated bad or illegal thing, although you have no proof
19. Shaped like a ball or circle
20. Unhappy or sorry

Puzzle #21

Across
1. Revealing
2. Able to produce the intended result
3. Not correct
4. Attractive in appearance
5. Containing, tasting of, or similar to nuts
6. Not clear and having no form

Down
7. Able to stretch
8. Coming before all others
9. Sing other people or situations as a way to get something you want, esp. in a selfish or secret way
10. Not dirty
11. Attractive or pleasant
12. Not bitter or salty

Puzzle #22

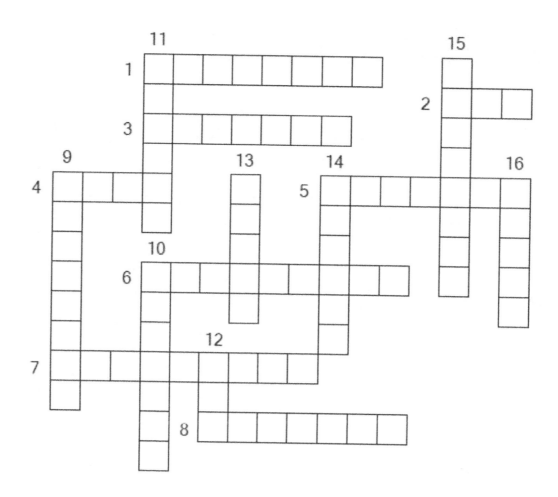

Across
1. Happy and positive
2. Large in size or amount
3. Not armed
4. Boring
5. Officer
6. Attractive or pleasant
7. Limited to only one person
8. Refusing to obey

Down
9. Careful not to attract too much attention
10. Revealing
11. Rounded in a pleasant and attractive way
12. Unhappy or sorry
13. Containing, tasting of, or similar to nuts
14. Fashionable and interesting
15. Abnormal, deviant, different
16. Telling not the true

Puzzle #23

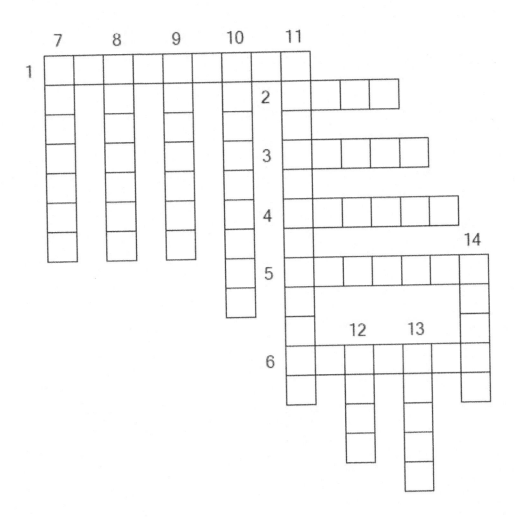

Across
1. Not wanting others to know
2. Not far away in distance
3. Feel slightly drunk
4. Not difficult
5. Worried, nervous
6. Extremely large

Down
7. Unusual and unexpected
8. Difficult to understand
9. Attractive in appearance
10. Gradually and secretly causing harm
11. Feeling of energetic interest
12. Man
13. Containing, tasting of, or similar to nuts
14. Not bitter or salty

Puzzle #24

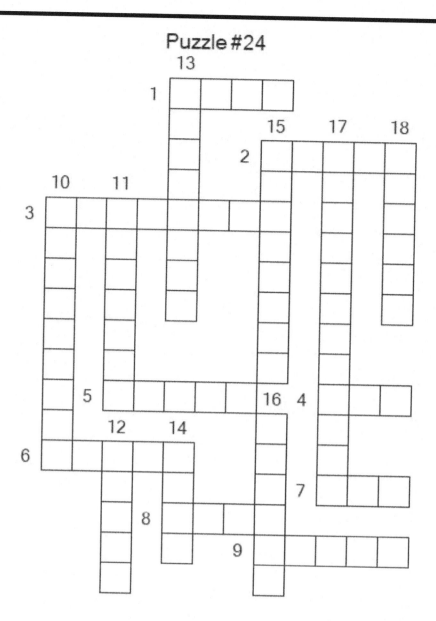

Across
1. Not in danger or likely to be harmed
2. Drinking too much alcohol
3. Without a home
4. Unhappy or sorry
5. Feel slightly drunk
6. Hard or firm
7. No water or other liquid in
8. Dissolves materials
9. Develop

Down
10. Extremely funny
11. Gigantic prehistoric animal
12. At the same height
13. Ability to do an activity or job well
14. Boring
15. Careful not to attract too much attention
16. Happening or done quickly and without warning
17. Not excited
18. Complicated and difficult to solve

Puzzle #25

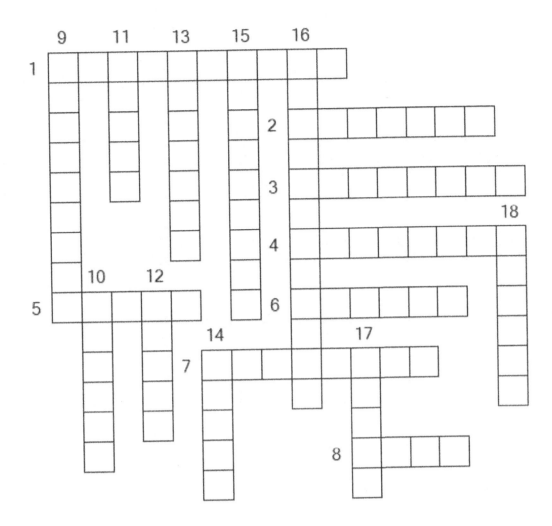

Across
1. Very pleasant
2. Extremely large
3. Happy or grateful because of something
4. Relating to love or a close loving relationship
5. Develop
6. Immediately after the first and before any others
7. Happy and positive
8. Not in danger or likely to be harmed

Down
9. Broken part
10. Strong and unlikely to break or fail
11. At the same height
12. Not dirty
13. Complain in an angry way
14. Causing pain intentionally
15. Attractive or pleasant
16. Not excited
17. Coming before all others
18. Rounded in a pleasant and attractive way

Puzzle #26

Across
1. Revealing
2. Gigantic prehistoric animal
3. Poor, unsuccessful, the state of being extremely unhappy
4. Able to stretch

Down
5. Dark and dirty or difficult to see through
6. Extremely large
7. Attractive or pleasant
8. At the same height
9. Feel slightly drunk
10. Unusual and unexpected
11. Rounded in a pleasant and attractive way
12. Containing, tasting of, or similar to nuts

Puzzle #27

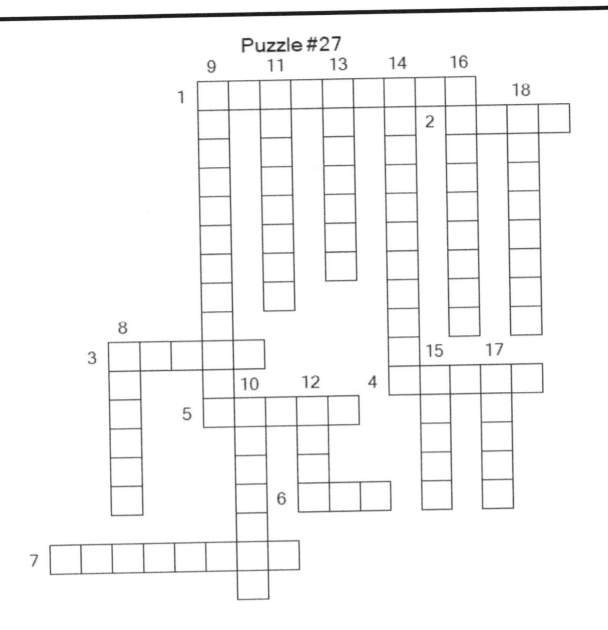

Across
1. Limited to only one person
2. Not far away in distance
3. Containing, tasting of, or similar to nuts
4. Develop
5. Not dirty
6. No water or other liquid in
7. Careful not to attract too much attention

Down
8. Ordinary or usual
9. Feeling of energetic interest
10. Showing much knowledge
11. Happy and positive
12. Dissolves materials
13. Not armed
14. Eager to know a lot
15. Shaped like a ball or circle
16. Having a lot of energy
17. Unwilling to give information
18. Someone who is trying to become successful

Puzzle #28

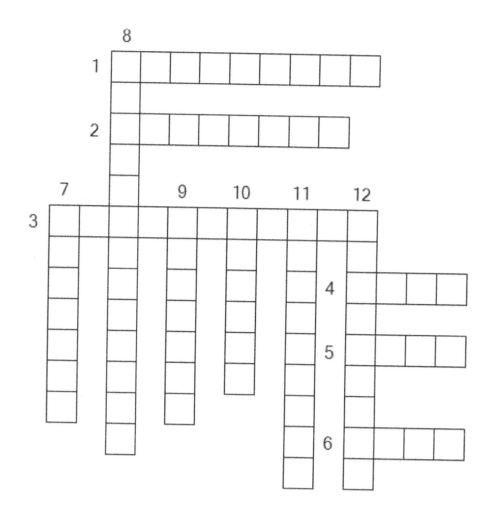

Across
1. Hing, or activity could harm you
2. Ability to do an activity or job well
3. Sing other people or situations as a way to get something you want, esp. in a selfish or secret way
4. Dissolves materials
5. Boring
6. Not in danger or likely to be harmed

Down
7. Difficult to understand
8. Disappointed discovering the truth
9. Not armed
10. Poor, unsuccessful, the state of being extremely unhappy
11. Gradually and secretly causing harm
12. Grand very large

Puzzle #29

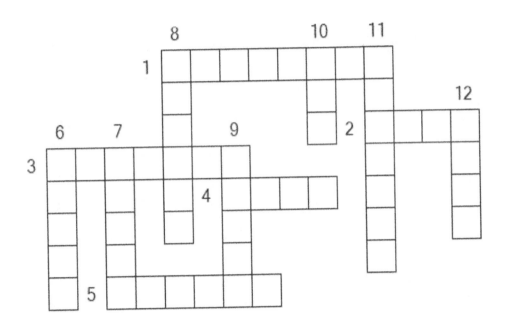

Across
1. Easily deceived
2. Dissolves materials
3. Extremely ugly or bad
4. Not physically strong
5. Complicated and difficult to solve

Down
6. Unkind, cruel
7. Drinking too much alcohol
8. Fashionable and interesting
9. Not bitter or salty
10. Unpleasant and causing difficulties or harm, evil, low quality, not acceptable
11. Able to stretch
12. Boring

Puzzle #30

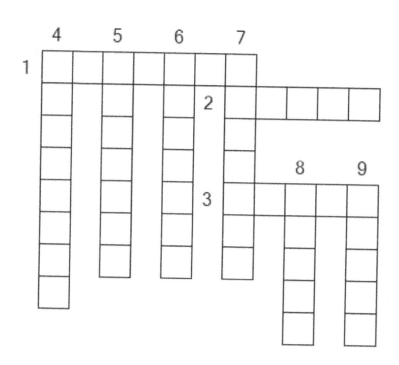

Across
1. Extremely surprising, very good, extremely surprised
2. Shaped like a ball or circle
3. Not dirty

Down
4. Excited, interested, enthusiastic
5. Worried, nervous
6. Extremely large
7. Complain in an angry way
8. Develop
9. Containing, tasting of, or similar to nuts

Puzzle #31

Across
1. Unhappy or sorry
2. Happy and positive
3. Large in size or amount
4. Containing, tasting of, or similar to nuts
5. Develop
6. Careful not to attract too much attention
7. Complicated and difficult to solve
8. No water or other liquid in

Down
9. Rounded in a pleasant and attractive way
10. Drinking too much alcohol
11. Not bitter or salty
12. Shaped like a ball or circle
13. Not excited
14. Causing pain intentionally

Puzzle #32

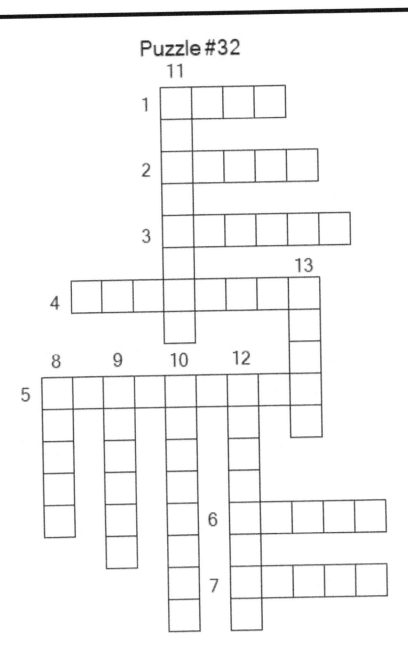

Across
1. Boring
2. Hard or firm
3. Strong and unlikely to break or fail
4. Without a home
5. Eager to fight or argue
6. Causing pain intentionally
7. Containing, tasting of, or similar to nuts

Down
8. Not dirty
9. Behave like adults
10. Abnormal, deviant, different
11. Careful not to attract too much attention
12. Not guilty of a particular crime
13. Not bitter or salty

Puzzle #33

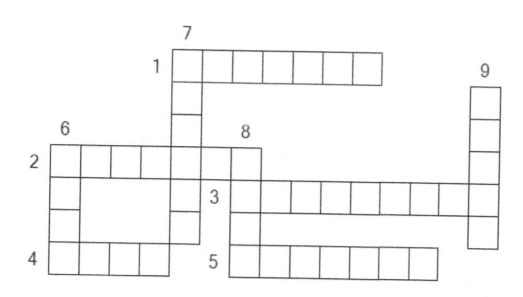

Across
1. Complain in an angry way
2. Worried, nervous
3. Detestable, repugnant, repulsive, morally very bad
4. Loved very much
5. Attractive in appearance

Down
6. Dissolves materials
7. Fashionable and interesting
8. Not in danger or likely to be harmed
9. Containing, tasting of, or similar to nuts

Puzzle #34

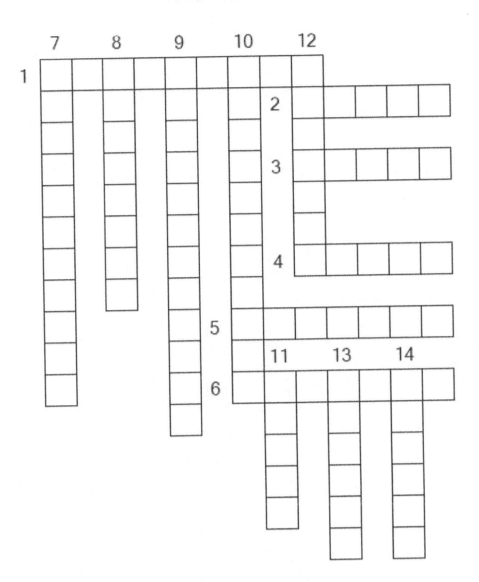

Across
1. Limited to only one person
2. Telling not the true
3. Not bitter or salty
4. Causing pain intentionally
5. Extremely large
6. Attractive in appearance

Down
7. Make something more likely to happen
8. Happy and positive
9. Not excited
10. Eager to know a lot
11. At the same height
12. Able to stretch
13. Fashionable and interesting
14. Ordinary or usual

Puzzle #35

Across
1. Glue
2. Ability to do an activity or job well
3. Poor, unsuccessful, the state of being extremely unhappy
4. Man
5. No water or other liquid in
6. Hard or firm

Down
7. Immediately after the first and before any others
8. Gradually and secretly causing harm
9. Said or thought by some people to be the stated bad or illegal thing, although you have no proof
10. Not armed
11. Not bitter or salty
12. Revealing

Puzzle #36

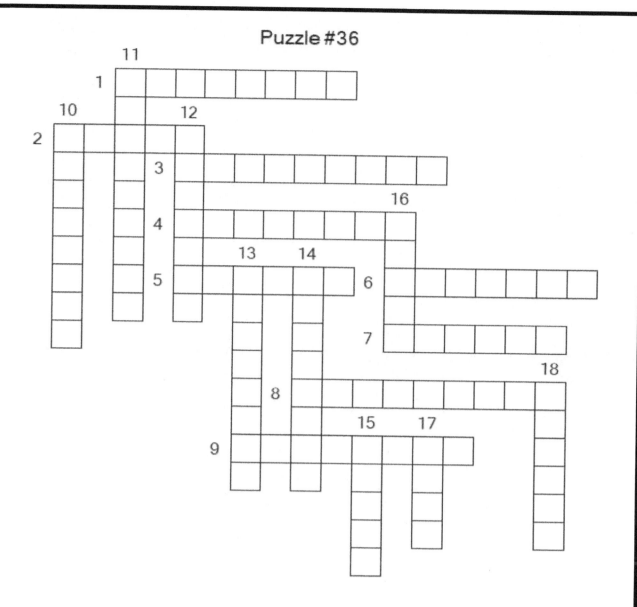

Across
1. Happy or grateful because of something
2. Having or showing respect for yourself
3. Having a lot of energy
4. Inside the body
5. Ordinary or usual
6. A foolish idea
7. Fashionable and interesting
8. Morally correct
9. Not guilty of aparticular crime

Down
10. Having a lot of power to control people and events
11. Attractive or pleasant
12. Refusing to obey
13. Relating to love or a close loving relationship
14. Someone who is trying to become successful
15. Causing pain intentionally
16. Telling not the true
17. Not far away in distance
18. Happening or done quickly and without warning

Puzzle #37

Across
1. Gradually and secretly causing harm
2. Extremely surprising, very good, extremely surprised
3. Behave like adults
4. Level and smooth
5. Make something more likely to happen
6. A foolish idea
7. Able to produce the intended result
8. Containing, tasting of, or similar to nuts

Down
9. Extremely large
10. Attractive or pleasant
11. Able to send back light a surface
12. Coming before all others
13. Unhappy or sorry
14. Causing pain intentionally
15. Fact that everyone knows
16. Not far away in distance
17. Immediately after the first and before any others

Puzzle #38

Across

1. Making you feel pleased by providing what you need or want
2. Poor, unsuccessful, the state of being extremely unhappy
3. Able to stretch
4. Extremely cold
5. At the same height
6. Not clear and having no form
7. Not in danger or likely to be harmed
8. Inside the body

Down

9. Worried, nervous
10. Someone who is trying to become successful
11. Not bitter or salty
12. Having a lot of energy
13. Revealing
14. Containing, tasting of, or similar to nuts
15. Damaged
16. Showing much knowledge
17. Not armed

Puzzle #39

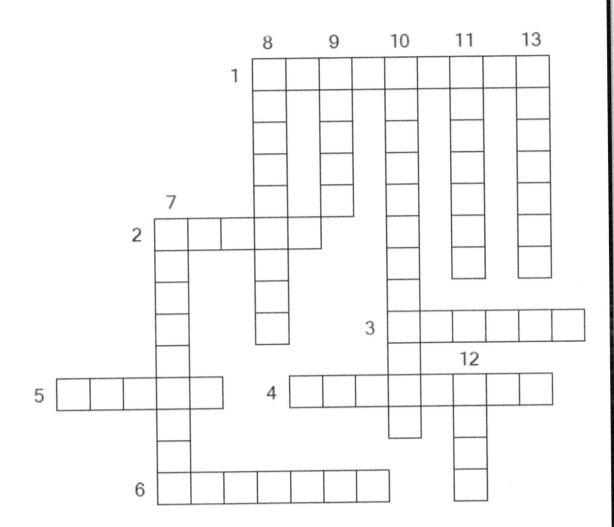

Across
1. Limited to only one person
2. Not bitter or salty
3. Rightened or worried
4. Happy and positive
5. Containing, tasting of, or similar to nuts
6. Able to stretch

Down
7. Not wanting others to know
8. Having a lot of energy
9. Unwilling to give information
10. Not excited
11. Extremely large
12. Level and smooth
13. Attractive in appearance

Puzzle #40

Across

1. Happening or done quickly and without warning
2. Not difficult
3. Strong and unlikely to break or fail
4. Not wanting others to know
5. Polite, honest, fair, and kind

Down

6. Rightened or worried
7. Fact that everyone knows
8. Develop
9. Hard or firm
10. Careful not to attract too much attention
11. Fashionable and interesting
12. Unhappy or sorry

Puzzle #41

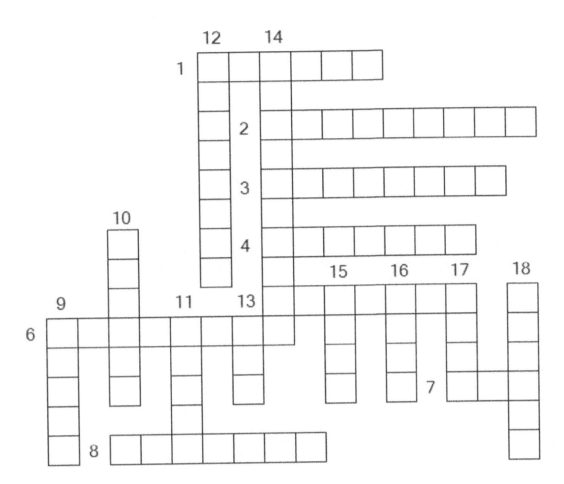

Across
1. Fashionable and interesting
2. Attractive or pleasant
3. Abnormal, deviant, different
4. Able to stretch
5. Not armed
6. Without a home
7. Unpleasant and causing difficulties or unusual harm, evil, low quality, not acceptable
8. Said or thought by some people to be the stated bad or illegal thing, although you have no proof

Down
9. Unkind, cruel
10. Fact that everyone knows
11. At the same height
12. Expressing thanks
13. Unhappy or sorry
14. Unacceptable, offensive, violent, or unusual
15. Dissolves materials
16. Nothing more than
17. Boring
18. Happening or done quickly and without warning

Puzzle #42

Across
1. On or onto a ship, aircraft, bus, or train
2. Without a home
3. Not decorated in any way; with nothing added
4. Shaped like a ball or circle
5. Containing, tasting of, or similar to nuts
6. Dissolves materials
7. Level and smooth
8. Revealing

Down
9. Stopping and starting repeatedly
10. Beautiful, powerful, or causing great admiration and respect
11. Feeling of energetic interest
12. Someone who is trying to become successful
13. Not bitter or salty
14. Happy or grateful because of something
15. Respecting God

Puzzle #43

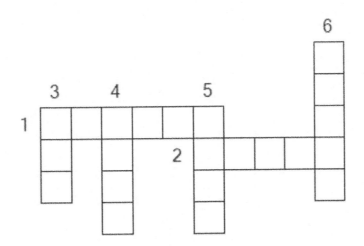

Across
1. Happening or done quickly and without warning
2. Develop

Down
3. Unhappy or sorry
4. Loved very much
5. Not far away in distance
6. Containing, tasting of, or similar to nuts

Puzzle #44

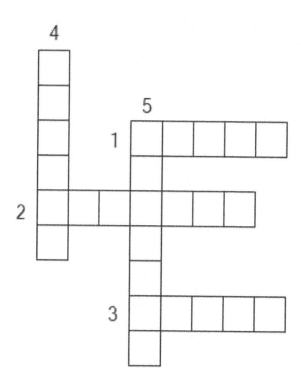

Across
1. Unkind, cruel
2. Revealing
3. Containing, tasting of, or similar to nuts

Down
4. Complicated and difficult to solve
5. Stopping and starting repeatedly

Puzzle #45

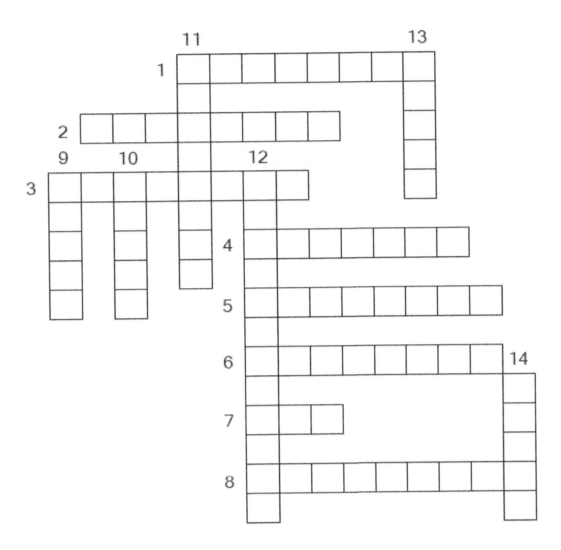

Across
1. Glue
2. Happy and positive
3. Having a lot of power to control people and events
4. A foolish idea
5. Happy or grateful because of something
6. Relating to love or a close loving relationship
7. Unhappy or sorry
8. Limited to only one person

Down
9. Not decorated in any way; with nothing added
10. Complete or not divided
11. Abnormal, deviant, different
12. Not excited
13. Develop
14. Not bitter or salty

Puzzle #46

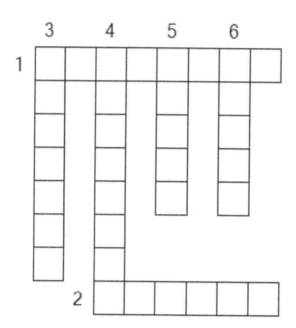

Across
1. Not guilty of a particular crime
2. Not difficult

Down
3. A foolish idea
4. Not clear and having no form
5. Not dirty
6. Containing, tasting of, or similar to nuts

Puzzle #47

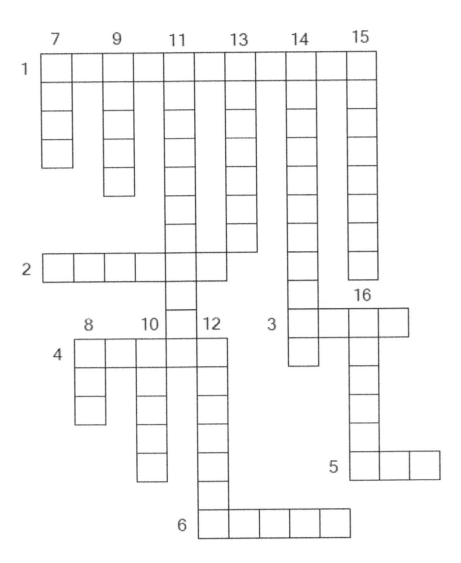

Across
1. Disapproving, wishing to fight or argue
2. Complicated and difficult to solve
3. Not far away in distance
4. Not bitter or salty
5. No water or other liquid in
6. Respecting God

Down
7. Most excellent, highest quality,
8. Unhappy or sorry
9. At the same height
10. Develop
11. Eager to know a lot
12. Revealing
13. Attractive in appearance
14. Make something more likely to happen
15. Happy or grateful because of something
16. On or onto a ship, aircraft, bus, or train

Puzzle #48

Across
1. Unkind, cruel
2. Gigantic prehistoric animal
3. At the same height
4. Hard or firm
5. Unacceptable, offensive, violent, or unusual
6. Stupid, unreasonable, silly in a humorous way, things that happen that are unreasonable
7. Nothing more than
8. Unhappy or sorry
9. No water or other liquid in

Down
10. Fashionable and interesting
11. Complicated and difficult to solve
12. Worried, nervous
13. Happy and positive
14. Not armed
15. Without a home
16. Boring

Puzzle #49

Across
1. Not in danger or likely to be harmed
2. The color of chocolate
3. Attractive in appearance
4. Said or thought by some people to be the stated bad or illegal thing, although you have no proof
5. Unusual and unexpected
6. Complicated and difficult to solve

Down
7. Large and strong
8. Unacceptable, offensive, violent, or unusual
9. Not clear and having no form
10. Strong and unlikely to break or fail
11. Containing, tasting of, or similar to nuts
12. Not bitter or salty
13. Boring
14. Revealing

Puzzle #50

Across
1. Containing, tasting of, or similar to nuts
2. Eager to know a lot
3. Telling not the true
4. Boring
5. Respecting God
6. Not far away in distance
7. No water or other liquid in

Down
8. Not guilty of a particular crime
9. Not armed
10. Happening or done quickly and without warning
11. Develop
12. Complicated and difficult to solve
13. Shaped like a ball or circle
14. Attractive in appearance
15. Refusing to obey

Puzzle #51

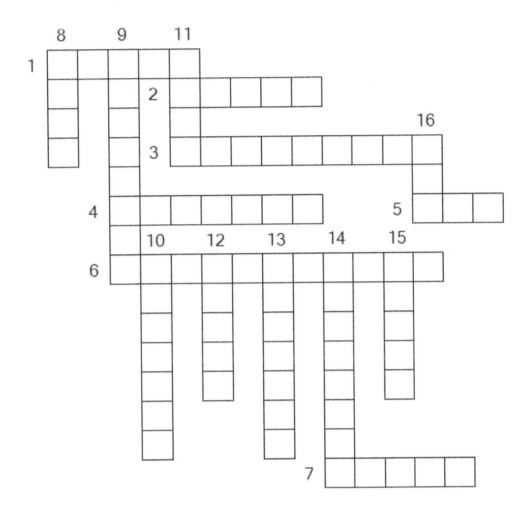

Across

1. Not decorated in any way; with nothing added
2. Develop
3. Morally correct
4. Revealing
5. No water or other liquid in
6. Sing other people or situations as a way to get something you want, esp. in a selfish or secret way
7. Telling not the true

Down

8. Having less color than usual
9. Having a pleasant smell
10. Worried, nervous
11. Not far away in distance
12. Not dirty
13. Showing much knowledge
14. Happy or grateful because of something
15. Containing, tasting of, or similar to nuts
16. Unhappy or sorry

Puzzle #52

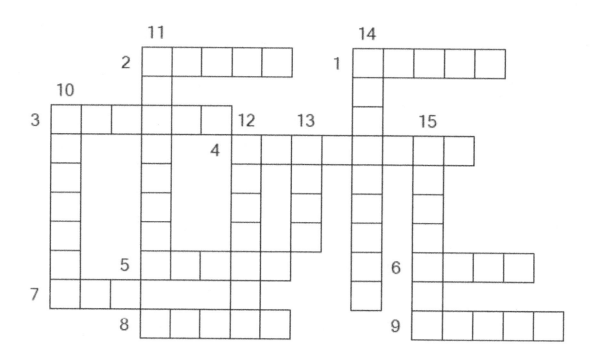

Across
1. Respecting God
2. Feel slightly drunk
3. Fact that everyone knows
4. Having a lot of power to control people and events
5. Not bitter or salty
6. Man
7. No water or other liquid in
8. Containing, tasting of, or similar to nuts
9. Drinking too much alcohol

Down
10. Full of people
11. Without a home
12. Complete and correct in every way, of the best possible type or without fault
13. Not physically strong
14. Habit of talking a lot
15. Not armed

Puzzle #53

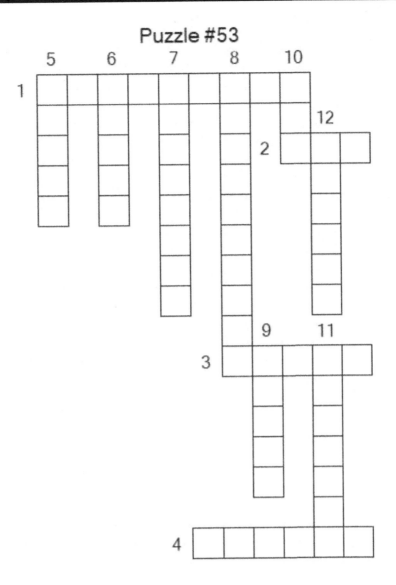

Across
1. Extremely funny
2. No water or other liquid in
3. Not bitter or salty
4. Complicated and difficult to solve

Down
5. Unkind, cruel
6. At the same height
7. Relating to love or a close loving relationship
8. Unacceptable, offensive, violent, or unusual
9. Complete or not divided
10. Unhappy or sorry
11. Attractive in appearance
12. Strong and unlikely to break or fail

Puzzle #54

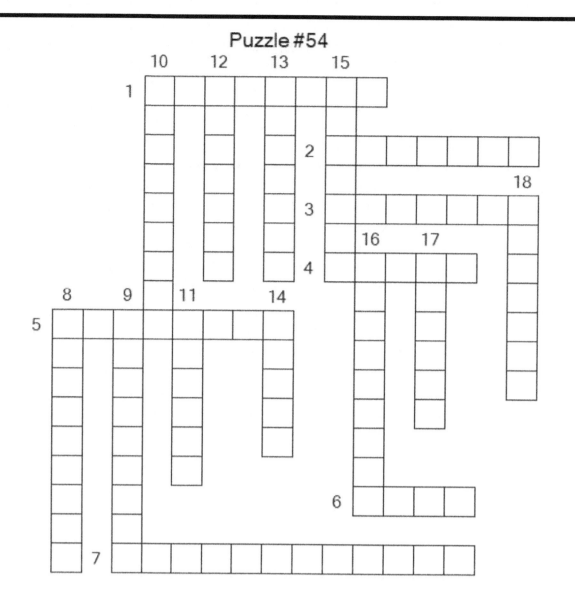

Across
1. Ability to do an activity or job well
2. Worried, nervous
3. Gigantic prehistoric animal
4. Drinking too much alcohol
5. Happy and positive
6. Not in danger or likely to be harmed
7. Feeling of energetic interest

Down
8. Eager to fight or argue
9. Limited to only one person
10. Not wanting others to know
11. Strong and unlikely to break or fail
12. Extremely large
13. Showing much knowledge
14. Telling not the true
15. Not armed
16. Morally correct
17. Ordinary or usual
18. Stopping and starting repeatedly

Puzzle #55

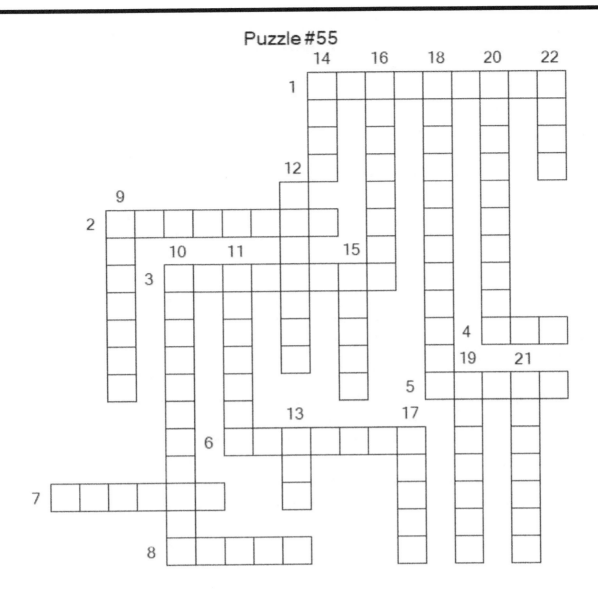

Across
1. Hing, or activity could harm you
2. Careful not to attract too much attention
3. Without a home
4. Unhappy or sorry
5. Unwilling to give information
6. Extremely ugly or bad
7. Complicated and difficult to solve
8. Containing, tasting of, or similar to nuts

Down
9. Refusing to obey
10. Trying to seem very important
11. Gigantic prehistoric animal
12. Revealing
13. No water or other liquid in
14. Boring
15. Not bitter or salty
16. Not clear and having no form
17. Hard or firm
18. Feeling of energetic interest
19. Said or thought by some people to be the stated bad or illegal thing, although you have no proof
20. Unacceptable, offensive, violent, or unusual
21. Able to stretch
22. Not in danger or likely to be harmed

Puzzle #56

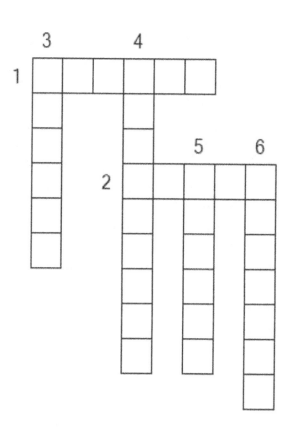

Across
1. Happening or done quickly and without warning
2. Coming before all others

Down
3. Not difficult
4. Not the same
5. Strong and unlikely to break or fail
6. Revealing

Puzzle #57

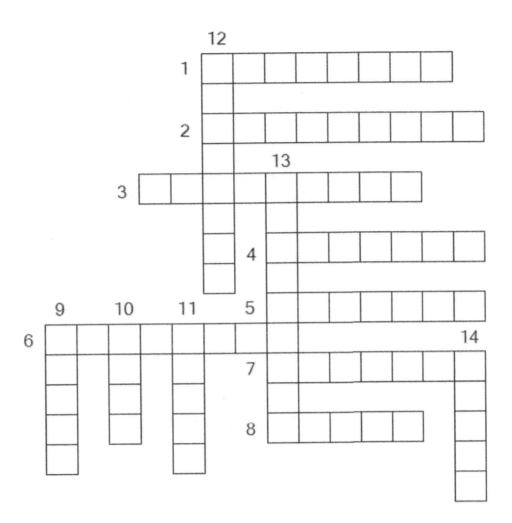

Across
1. Attractive, appealing, lovely, charming, and easily loved
2. Having a lot of energy
3. Accepted, accept something
4. Unkind, cruel, without sympathy
5. Not armed
6. Without a home
7. A foolish idea
8. Develop

Down
9. Feel slightly drunk
10. Man
11. At the same height
12. Abnormal, deviant, different
13. Limited to only one person
14. Unwilling to give information

Puzzle #58

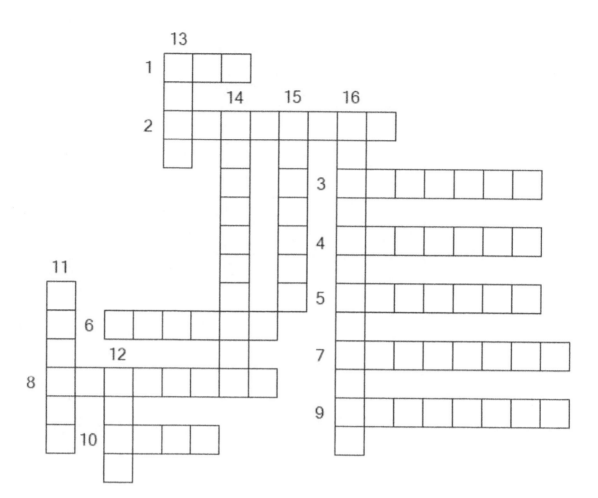

Across
1. No water or other liquid in
2. Excited, interested, enthusiastic
3. Revealing
4. Not armed
5. A foolish idea
6. Rounded in a pleasant and attractive way
7. Ability to do an activity or job well
8. Careful not to attract too much attention
9. Not guilty of a particular crime
10. Level and smooth

Down
11. Happening or done quickly and without warning
12. Not in danger or likely to be harmed
13. Boring
14. Impossible to defeat
15. Worried, nervous
16. Feeling of energetic interest

Puzzle #59

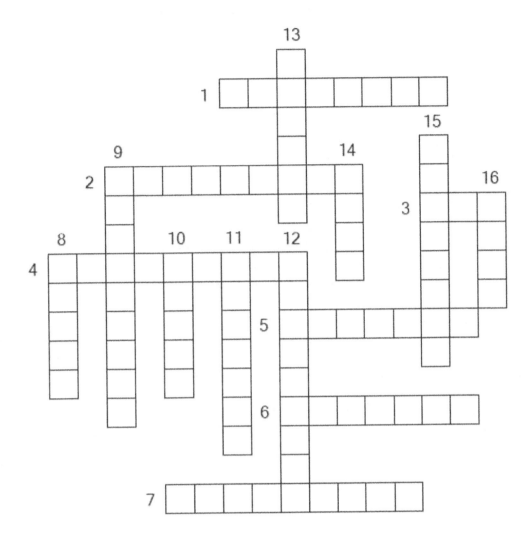

Across
1. Not guilty of aparticular crime
2. Feeling extreme dislike
3. Unhappy or sorry
4. Broken part
5. Difficult to understand
6. Unusual and unexpected
7. Accepted, accept something

Down
8. Drinking too much alcohol
9. Not the same
10. Unwilling to give information
11. A foolish idea
12. Limited to only one person
13. Complicated and difficult to solve
14. Boring
15. Careful not to attract too much attention
16. Loved very much

Solutions

Puzzle #1

Across
1. Dissolves materials
2. Loved very much
3. Ordinary
4. Respecting God
5. Without a home
6. Boring
7. Beautiful, powerful, or causing great admiration and respect
8. Very respected
9. Unhappy or sorry
10. Not in danger or likely to be harmed

Down
11. Extremely ugly or bad
12. On or onto a ship, aircraft, bus, or train
13. Man
14. Unkind, cruel
15. Careful not to attract too much attention
16. Coming before all others
17. Very well
18. Dark and dirty or difficult to see through
19. Not having something
20. Said or thought by some people to be the stated bad or illegal thing, although you have no proof
21. Refusing to obey
22. Extremely large
23. No water or other liquid in

Puzzle #2

Across
1. Not certain, or wrong in some way
2. Unhappy or sorry
3. Having a lot of energy
4. Easy to understand
5. Containing, tasting of, or similar to nuts

Down
6. Not excited
7. Hard or firm
8. Develop
9. Extremely large
10. Not clear and having no form
11. Damaged
12. Not dirty
13. Feeling of energetic interest

Puzzle #3

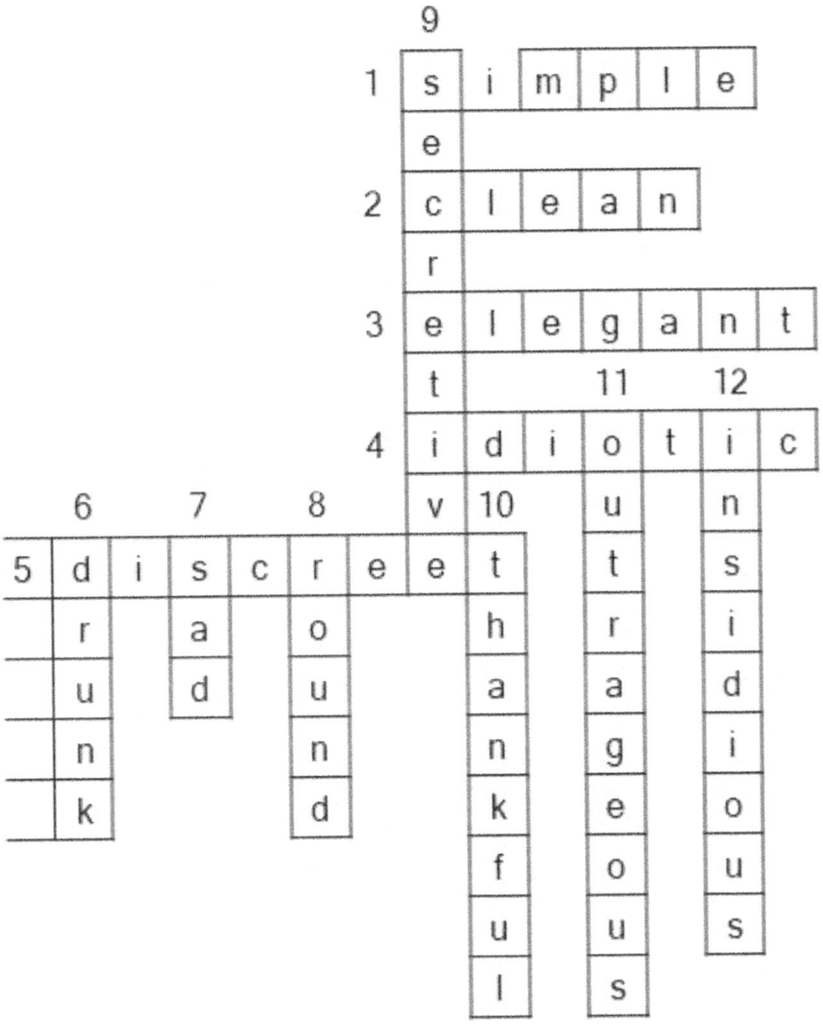
9
1 s i m p l e
e
2 c l e a n
r
3 e l e g a n t
t 11 12
4 i d i o t i c
6 7 8 v 10 u n
5 d i s c r e e t t s
r a o h r i
u d u a a d
n n n g i
k d k e o
f o u
u u s
l s

Across

1. Not difficult
2. Not dirty
3. Attractive in appearance
4. A foolish idea
5. Careful not to attract too much attention

Down

6. Drinking too much alcohol
7. Unhappy or sorry
8. Shaped like a ball or circle
9. Not wanting others to know
10. Happy or grateful because of something
11. Unacceptable, offensive, violent, or unusual
12. Gradually and secretly causing harm

Puzzle #4

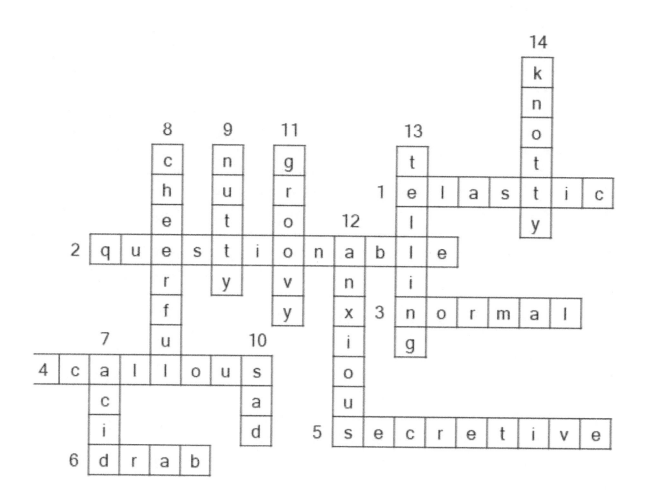

Across
1. Able to stretch
2. Not certain, or wrong in some way
3. Ordinary or usual
4. Unkind, cruel, without sympathy
5. Not wanting others to know
6. Boring

Down
7. Dissolves materials
8. Happy and positive
9. Containing, tasting of, or similar to nuts
10. Unhappy or sorry
11. Fashionable and interesting
12. Worried, nervous
13. Revealing
14. Complicated and difficult to solve

Puzzle #5

1. amazing (Across)
2. majestic (Across)
3. handsome (Across)
4. robust (Across)
5. level (Across)

6. immense (Down)
7. elegant (Down)
8. Mass (Down)
9. selling (Down)
10. cheerful (Down)
11. lying (Down)
12. common (Down)

Across
1. Extremely surprising, very good, extremely surprised
2. Beautiful, powerful, or causing great admiration and respect
3. Physically attractive
4. Strong and unlikely to break or fail
5. At the same height

Down
6. Extremely large
7. Attractive in appearance
8. The amount of matter in an object
9. Revealing
10. Happy and positive
11. Telling not the true
12. Fact that everyone knows

Puzzle #6

```
                    7
                 1  d   r   y
                    i
                    s
                    i
                    l
                    l
                    u
                    s
                    i
              2  g  r   o   o   v   y
                 6          n
              3  s  w   e   e   t
                 c          d
                 a
        4  g  a  r  r   u   l   o   u   s
                 e
     5  s  u  d  d   e   n
```

Across
1. No water or other liquid in
2. Fashionable and interesting
3. Not bitter or salty
4. Habit of talking a lot
5. Happening or done quickly and without warning

Down
6. Rightened or worried
7. Disappointed discovering the truth

Puzzle #7

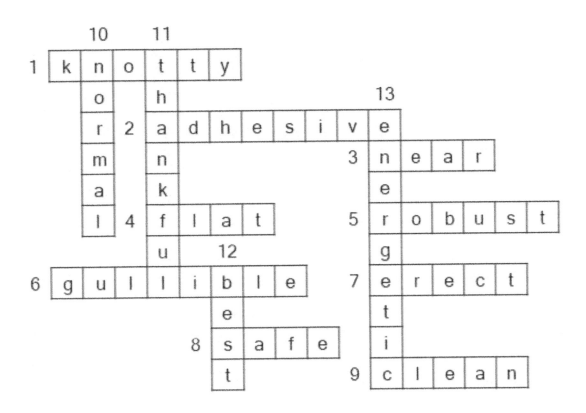

Across
1. Complicated and difficult to solve
2. Glue
3. Not far away in distance
4. Level and smooth
5. Strong and unlikely to break or fail
6. Easily deceived
7. Develop
8. Not in danger or likely to be harmed
9. Not dirty

Down
10. Ordinary or usual
11. Happy or grateful because of something
12. Most excellent, highest quality,
13. Having a lot of energy

Puzzle #8

```
                    9
      1 k n o t t y
              8     o     10     11
        2 a r o m a t i c
          n     t     m     n
          x     h     a 3 n o r m a l
          i     s     z     o
          o     o     i 4 c l o u d y
          u     m     n     e     12
          s     e     g 5 n e a r
                        t     b
                              h
                              o
                              r
                              r
                    6 s w e e t
                              n
                    7 n u t t y
```

Across
1. Complicated and difficult to solve
2. Having a pleasant smell
3. Ordinary or usual
4. With clouds
5. Not far away in distance
6. Not bitter or salty
7. Containing, tasting of, or similar to nuts

Down
8. Worried, nervous
9. Attractive or pleasant
10. Extremely surprising, very good, extremely surprised
11. Not guilty of a particular crime
12. Detestable, repugnant, repulsive, morally very bad

Puzzle #9

Crossword grid:

Across
1. aboard
2. homeless
3. dry
4. common
5. nebulous
6. internal

Grid letters filled in:
- 1 (across): a b o a r d
- 2 (across): h o m e l e s s
- 3 (across): d r y
- 4 (across): c o m m o n
- 5 (across): n e b u l o u s
- 6 (across): i n t e r n a l
- 7 (down): h o m e l y
- 8 (down): m a l e
- 9 (down): c h u b b y
- 10 (down): l e a r n e d
- 11 (down): r o
- 12 (down): b s u r d (absurd)
- 13 (down): a r o m a t i c
- 14 (down): d e a r

Across
1. On or onto a ship, aircraft, bus, or train
2. Without a home
3. No water or other liquid in
4. Fact that everyone knows
5. Not clear and having no form
6. Inside the body

Down
7. Ordinary
8. Man
9. Rounded in a pleasant and attractive way
10. Showing much knowledge
11. Relating to love or a close loving relationship
12. Stupid, unreasonable, silly in a humorous way, things that happen that are unreasonable
13. Having a pleasant smell
14. Loved very much

Puzzle #10

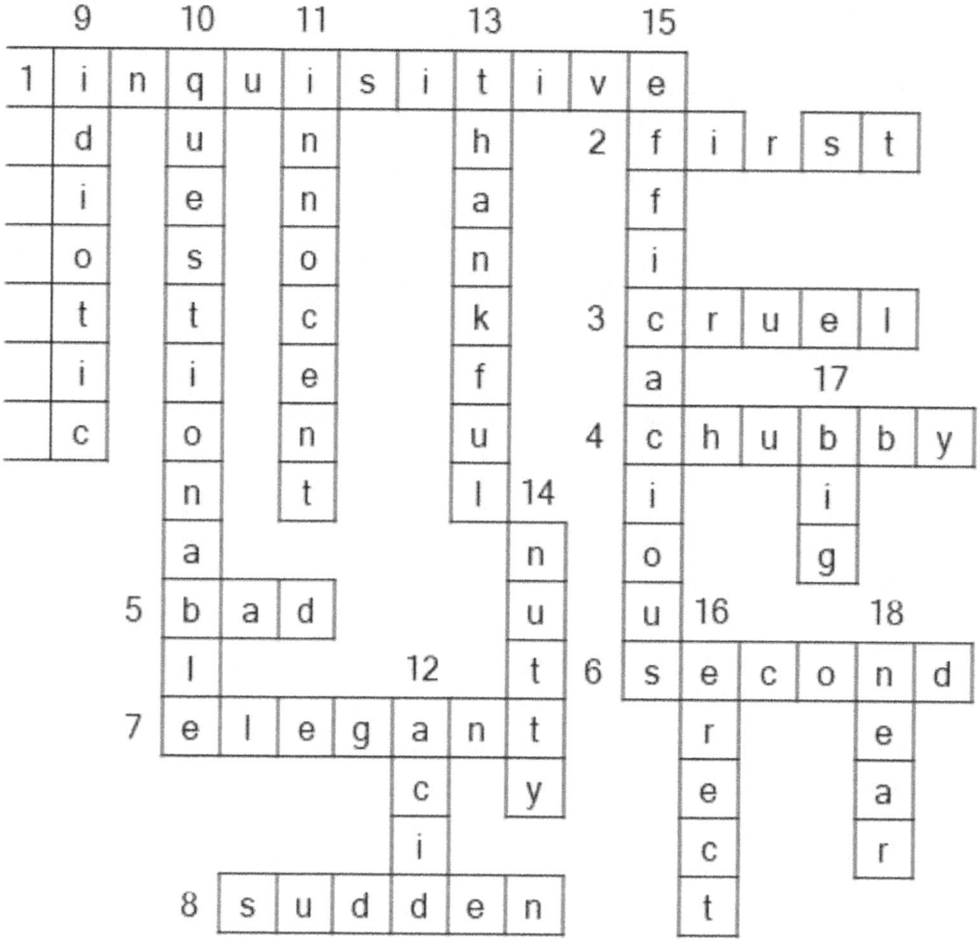

A crossword grid with the following entries:

Across
- 1. inquisitive
- 2. first
- 3. cruel
- 4. chubby
- 5. bad
- 6. second
- 7. elegant
- 8. sudden

Down
- 9. idiotic
- 10. unsustion (grid letters: q u e s t i o n a b l e)
- 11. innocent
- 12. acid
- 13. thankful
- 14. nutty
- 15. effective (grid letters: e f f i c a c i o u s)
- 16. erect
- 17. big
- 18. near

Across
1. Eager to know a lot
2. Coming before all others
3. Causing pain intentionally
4. Rounded in a pleasant and attractive way
5. Unpleasant and causing difficulties or harm, evil, low quality, not acceptable
6. Immediately after the first and before any others
7. Attractive in appearance
8. Happening or done quickly and without warning

Down
9. A foolish idea
10. Not certain, or wrong in some way
11. Not guilty of a particular crime
12. Dissolves materials
13. Happy or grateful because of something
14. Containing, tasting of, or similar to nuts
15. Able to produce the intended result
16. Develop
17. Large in size or amount
18. Not far away in distance

Puzzle #11

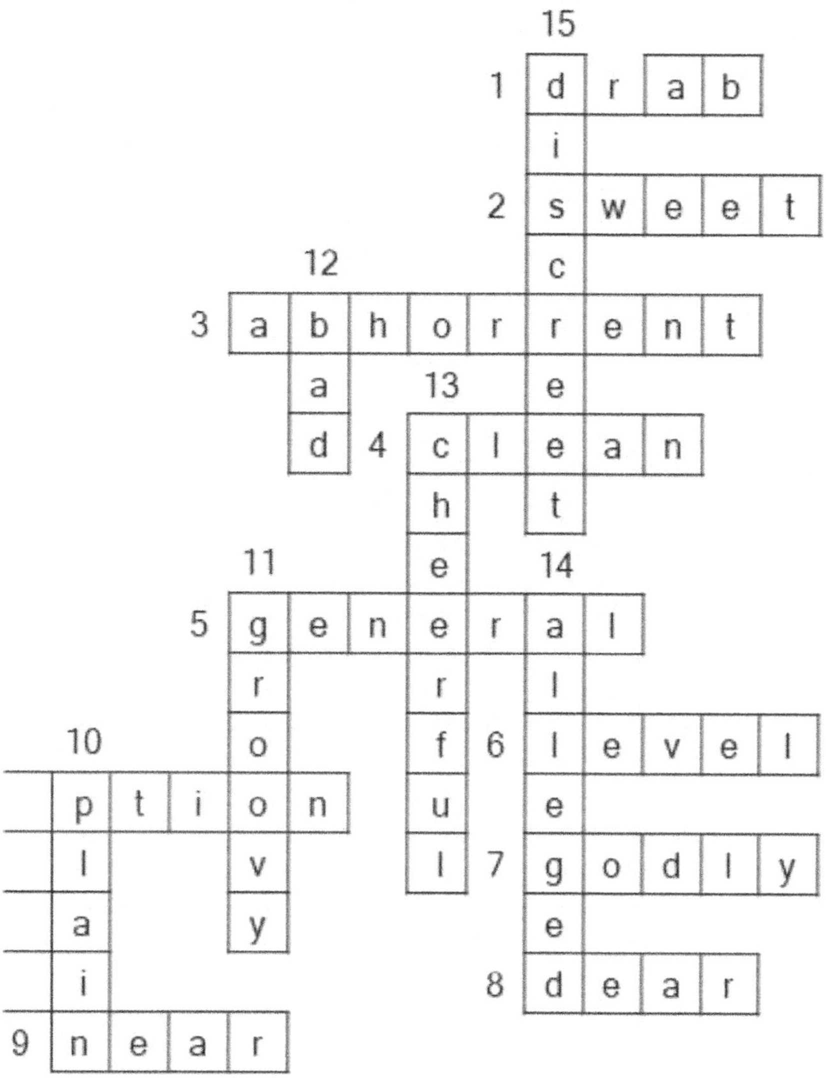

		15			
1	d	r	a	b

(Crossword grid)

1. d r a b
15 (down): d i s c r e e t
2. s w e e t
12 (down): b a d
3. a b h o r r e n t
13 (down): c h e e r f u l
4. c l e a n
11 (down): g r o o v y
5. g e n e r a l
14 (down): a l l e g e d
6. l e v e l
10. p t i o n
7. g o d l y
8. d e a r
9. n e a r

Across
1. Boring
2. Not bitter or salty
3. Detestable, repugnant, repulsive, morally very bad
4. Not dirty
5. Officer
6. At the same height
7. Respecting God
8. Loved very much
9. Not far away in distance

Down
10. Not decorated in any way; with nothing added
11. Fashionable and interesting
12. Unpleasant and causing difficulties or harm, evil, low quality, not acceptable
13. Happy and positive
14. Said or thought by some people to be the stated bad or illegal thing, although you have no proof
15. Careful not to attract too much attention

Puzzle #12

	5		6		7			9						13
1	t	o	o	t	h	s	o	m	e					
	h		u		i			a						d
	a		t		l	2	l	y	i	n	g			i
	n		r		a			e						s
	k		a		r									c
	f		g	3	i	n	s	i	d	i	o	u	s	r
	u		e		o		8		10		11		12	e
	l		o	4	u	n	i	n	t	e	r	e	s	t	e	d
			u		s		d		e		o		e	t
			s				i		l		b		c
							o		l		u		r
							t		i		s		e
							i		n		t		t
							c		g				i
													v
													e

Across
1. Attractive or pleasant
2. Telling not the true
3. Gradually and secretly causing harm
4. Not excited

Down
5. Happy or grateful because of something
6. Unacceptable, offensive, violent, or unusual
7. Extremely funny
8. A foolish idea
9. Man
10. Revealing
11. Strong and unlikely to break or fail
12. Not wanting others to know
13. Careful not to attract too much attention

Puzzle #13

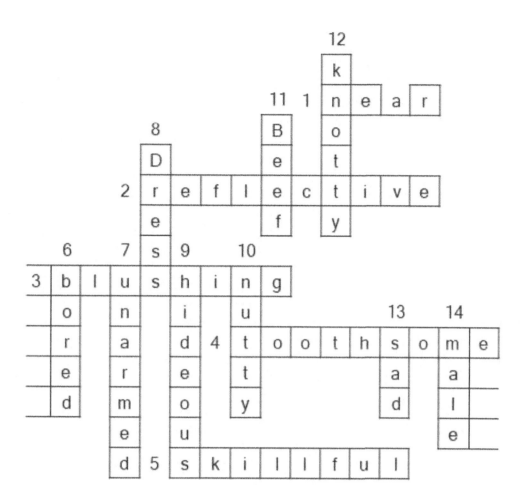

Across
1. Not far away in distance
2. Able to send back light a surface
3. Become pink in the face
4. Attractive or pleasant
5. Ability to do an activity or job well

Down
6. Unhappy because you have nothing to do
7. Not armed
8. Put on one's clothes
9. Extremely ugly or bad
10. Containing, tasting of, or similar to nuts
11. Flesh of a cow
12. Complicated and difficult to solve
13. Unhappy or sorry
14. Man

Puzzle #14

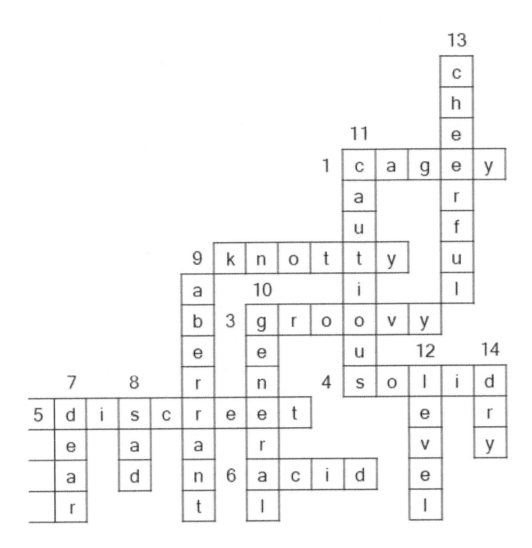

Across
1. Unwilling to give information
2. Complicated and difficult to solve
3. Fashionable and interesting
4. Hard or firm
5. Careful not to attract too much attention
6. Dissolves materials

Down
7. Loved very much
8. Unhappy or sorry
9. Abnormal, deviant, different
10. Officer
11. Avoids risks
12. At the same height
13. Happy and positive
14. No water or other liquid in

Puzzle #15

```
        10      11      12      14
   1 [a][s][p][i][r][i][n][g]                    18
      [b]   [a]   [i]   [o]                      [s]
      [e]   [l]   [g] 2[r][o][u][n][d]           [u]
      [r]   [e]   [h]   [m]                       [d]
      [r]         [t] 3[a][l][l][e][g][e][d]     [d]
    8 [r]         [e]   [l]                       [e]
   [i] [a]         [o]  15    16    17            [n]
   [n] [n]   4[n][u][t][t][y] 5[u][n][a][r][m][e][d]
             [o]              [s]  [b]  [a]  [r]
   6[c][l][e][a][n]               [o]  [t]  [u]
      [e]    9              13    [a]  [u]  [n]
   7[n][e][b][u][l][o][u][s]     [r]  [r]  [k]
      [t]   [i]              [a]  [d]  [e]
            [g]              [d]
```

Across

1. Someone who is trying to become successful
2. Shaped like a ball or circle
3. Said or thought by some people to be the stated bad or illegal thing, although you have no proof
4. Containing, tasting of, or similar to nuts
5. Not armed
6. Not dirty
7. Not clear and having no form

Down

8. Not guilty of a particular crime
9. Large in size or amount
10. Abnormal, deviant, different
11. Having less color than usual
12. Morally correct
13. Unhappy or sorry
14. Ordinary or usual
15. On or onto a ship, aircraft, bus, or train
16. Behave like adults
17. Drinking too much alcohol
18. Happening or done quickly and without warning

Puzzle #16

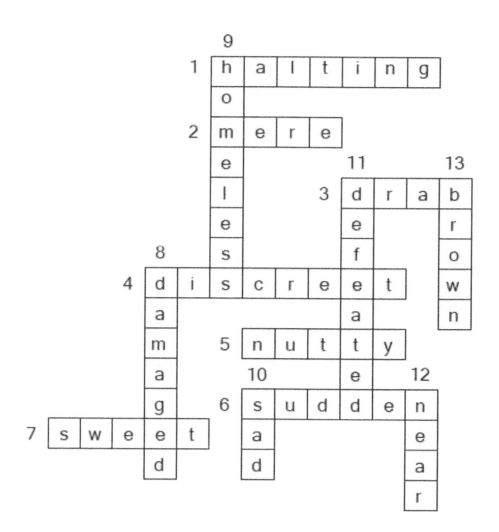

Across
1. Stopping and starting repeatedly
2. Nothing more than
3. Boring
4. Careful not to attract too much attention
5. Containing, tasting of, or similar to nuts
6. Happening or done quickly and without warning
7. Not bitter or salty

Down
8. Harmed or spoiled
9. Without a home
10. Unhappy or sorry
11. Losing against someone
12. Not far away in distance
13. The color of chocolate

Puzzle #17

Across: 1 callous, 2 drab, 3 outrageous, 4 internal, 5 thankful, 6 romantic, 7 sudden, 8 discreet, 9 defeated

Down: 10 toothsome, 11 telling, 12 dry, 13 abject, 14 solid, 15 cheerful, 16 round, 17 unfl (unfeel...), 19 sad, 21 common

Across
1. Unkind, cruel, without sympathy
2. Boring
3. Unacceptable, offensive, violent, or unusual
4. Inside the body
5. Happy or grateful because of something
6. Relating to love or a close loving relationship
7. Happening or done quickly and without warning
8. Careful not to attract too much attention
9. Losing against someone

Down
10. Attractive or pleasant
11. Revealing
12. No water or other liquid in
13. Poor, unsuccessful, the state of being extremely unhappy
14. Hard or firm
15. Happy and positive
16. Shaped like a ball or circle
17. Not excited
18. Drinking too much alcohol
19. Unhappy or sorry
20. Containing, tasting of, or similar to nuts
21. Fact that everyone knows

Puzzle #18

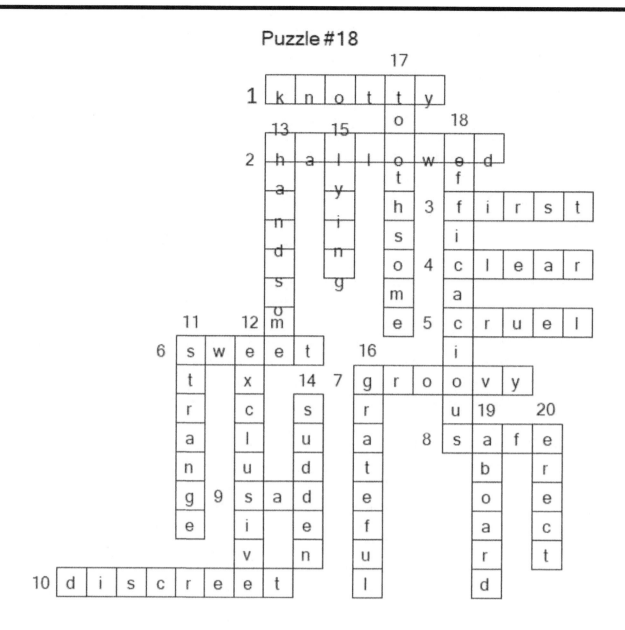

Across
1. Complicated and difficult to solve
2. Very respected
3. Coming before all others
4. Easy to understand
5. Causing pain intentionally
6. Not bitter or salty
7. Fashionable and interesting
8. Not in danger or likely to be harmed
9. Unhappy or sorry
10. Careful not to attract too much attention

Down
11. Unusual and unexpected
12. Limited to only one person
13. Physically attractive
14. Happening or done quickly and without warning
15. Telling not the true
16. Expressing thanks
17. Attractive or pleasant
18. Able to produce the intended result
19. On or onto a ship, aircraft, bus, or train
20. Develop

Puzzle #19

Across

1. Containing, tasting of, or similar to nuts
2. Rounded in a pleasant and attractive way
3. Telling not the true
4. Unhappy or sorry
5. Careful not to attract too much attention
6. Dissolves materials
7. Unkind, cruel, without sympathy

Down

8. Fact that everyone knows
9. Not armed
10. No water or other liquid in
11. Not clear and having no form
12. Happening or done quickly and without warning
13. Revealing
14. Shaped like a ball or circle
15. Extremely large
16. Happy or grateful because of something
17. Fashionable and interesting
18. Boring

Puzzle #20

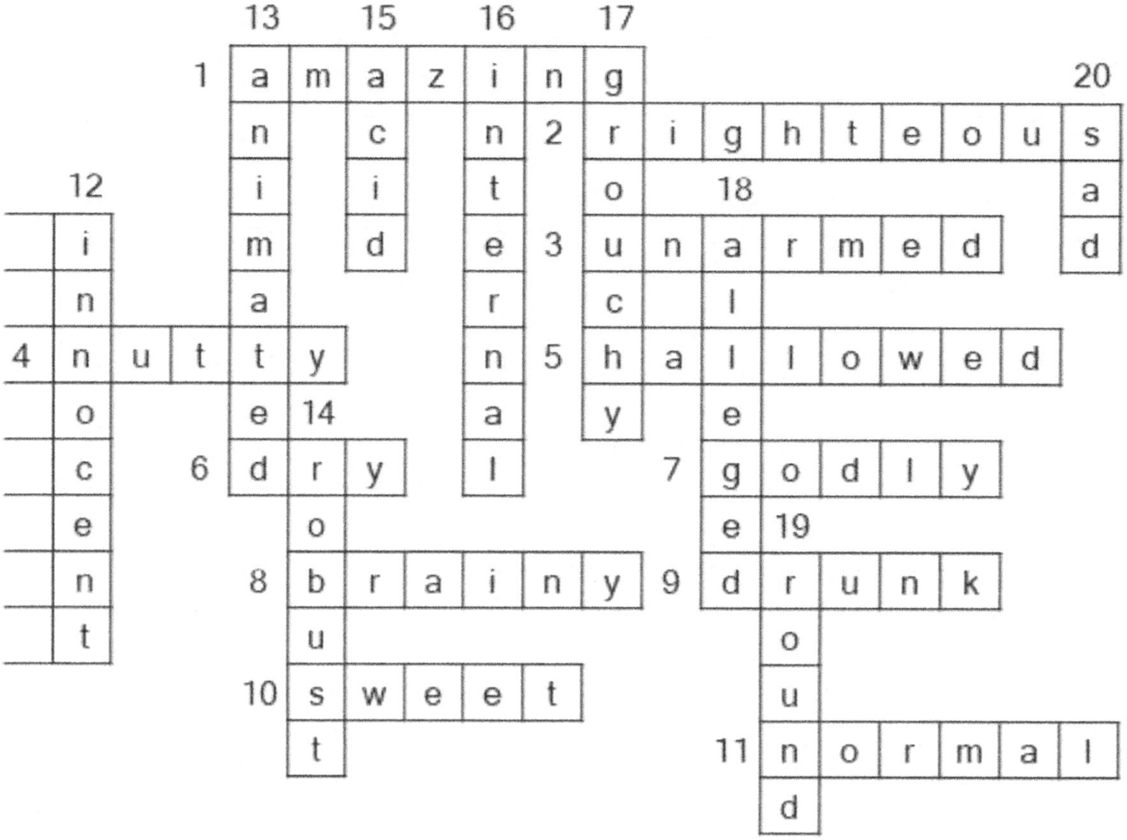

The crossword grid contains the following answers:

Across
1. amazing
2. righteous
3. unarmed
4. nutty
5. hallowed
6. dry
7. godly
8. brainy
9. drunk
10. sweet
11. normal

Down
12. innocent
13. animate
14. durable
15. acidic
16. internal
17. grounchy
18. allewed
19. round
20. sad

Across
1. Extremely surprising, very good, extremely surprised
2. Morally correct
3. Not armed
4. Containing, tasting of, or similar to nuts
5. Very respected
6. No water or other liquid in
7. Respecting God
8. Clever
9. Drinking too much alcohol
10. Not bitter or salty
11. Ordinary or usual

Down
12. Not guilty of aparticular crime
13. Excited, interested, enthusiastic
14. Strong and unlikely to break or fail
15. Dissolves materials
16. Inside the body
17. Complain in an angry way
18. Said or thought by some people to be the stated bad or illegal thing, although you have no proof
19. Shaped like a ball or circle
20. Unhappy or sorry

Puzzle #21

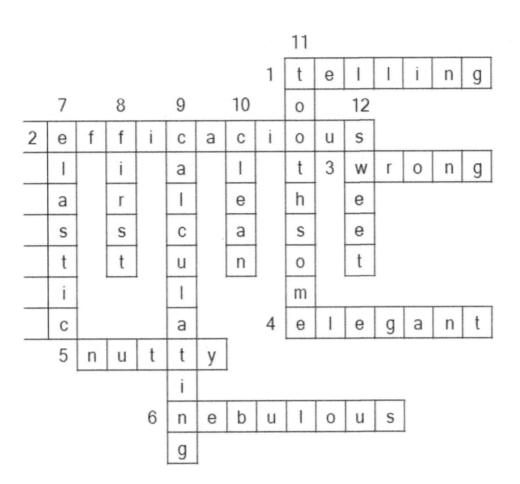

Across
1. Revealing
2. Able to produce the intended result
3. Not correct
4. Attractive in appearance
5. Containing, tasting of, or similar to nuts
6. Not clear and having no form

Down
7. Able to stretch
8. Coming before all others
9. Sing other people or situations as a way to get something you want, esp. in a selfish or secret way
10. Not dirty
11. Attractive or pleasant
12. Not bitter or salty

Puzzle #22

Across
1. cheerful
2. big
3. unarmed
4. drab
5. general
6. toothsome
7. exclusive
8. defiant

Down
9. discreet
10. telling
11. chubby
12. sad
13. nutty
14. groovy
15. aberrant
16. lying

Across
1. Happy and positive
2. Large in size or amount
3. Not armed
4. Boring
5. Officer
6. Attractive or pleasant
7. Limited to only one person
8. Refusing to obey

Down
9. Careful not to attract too much attention
10. Revealing
11. Rounded in a pleasant and attractive way
12. Unhappy or sorry
13. Containing, tasting of, or similar to nuts
14. Fashionable and interesting
15. Abnormal, deviant, different
16. Telling not the true

Puzzle #23

	7	8	9	10	11		
1	s	e	c	r	e	t	i	v	e

Grid letters:

1 Across: s e c r e t i v e
2 Across: n e a r
3 Across: h e a d y
4 Across: s i m p l e
5 Across: a n x i o u s
6 Across: i m m e n s e

7 Down: s t r a n g e
8 Down: c o m p l e x
9 Down: e l e g a n t
10 Down: i n s i d i o u s
11 Down: e n t h u s i a s t i c
12 Down: m a l e
13 Down: n u t t y
14 Down: s w e e t

Across
1. Not wanting others to know
2. Not far away in distance
3. Feel slightly drunk
4. Not difficult
5. Worried, nervous
6. Extremely large

Down
7. Unusual and unexpected
8. Difficult to understand
9. Attractive in appearance
10. Gradually and secretly causing harm
11. Feeling of energetic interest
12. Man
13. Containing, tasting of, or similar to nuts
14. Not bitter or salty

Puzzle #24

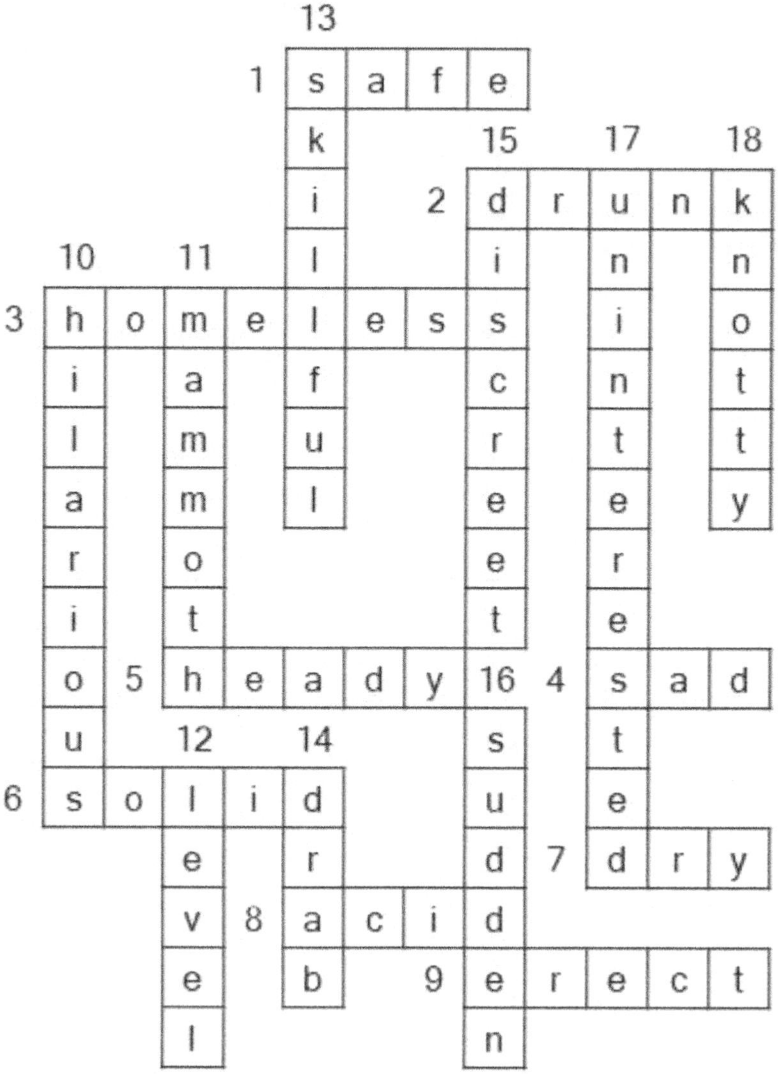

A crossword grid with the following entries:

Across:
1. safe
2. drunk
3. homeless
4. sad
5. heady
6. solid
7. dry
8. acid
9. erect

Down:
10. hilarious
11. mammoth
12. level
13. skill
14. dribble
15. discreet
16. sudden
17. uninterested
18. knotty

Across
1. Not in danger or likely to be harmed
2. Drinking too much alcohol
3. Without a home
4. Unhappy or sorry
5. Feel slightly drunk
6. Hard or firm
7. No water or other liquid in
8. Dissolves materials
9. Develop

Down
10. Extremely funny
11. Gigantic prehistoric animal
12. At the same height
13. Ability to do an activity or job well
14. Boring
15. Careful not to attract too much attention
16. Happening or done quickly and without warning
17. Not excited
18. Complicated and difficult to solve

Puzzle #25

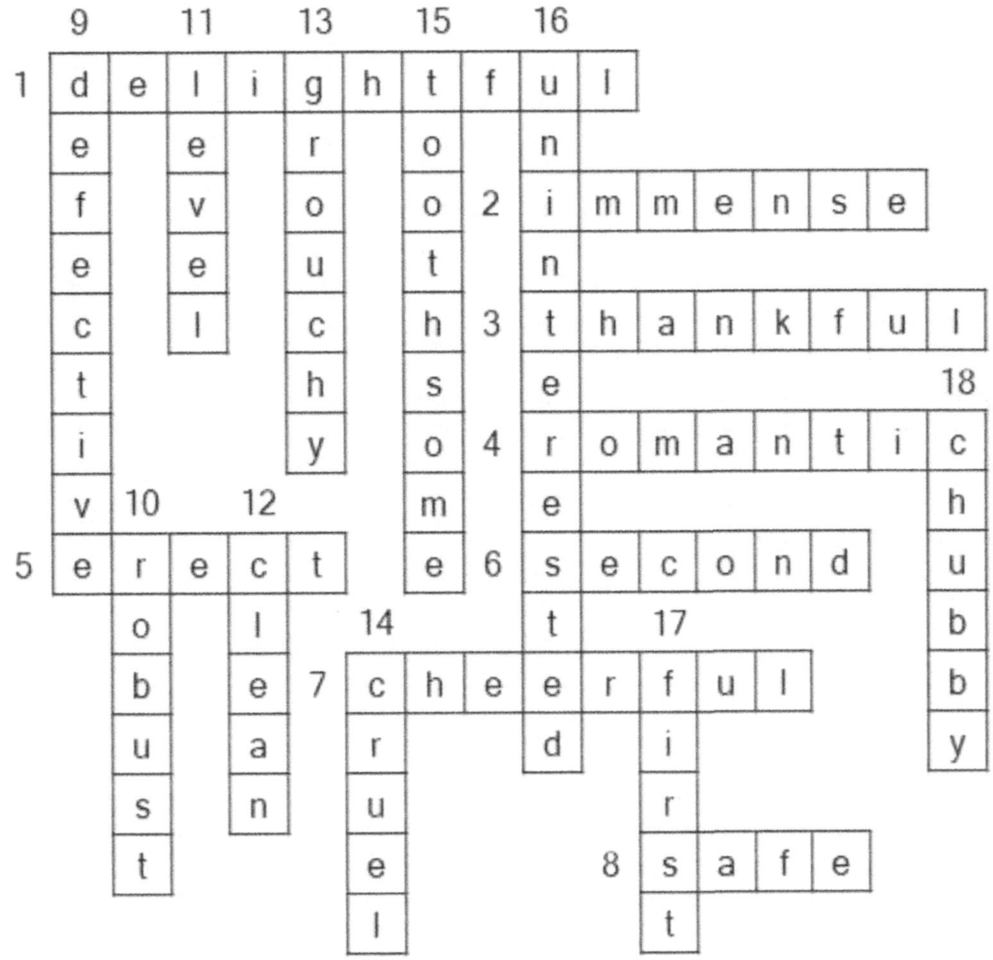

Across positions with numbers 9, 11, 13, 15, 16 at top.

1. d e l i g h t f u l
2. i m m e n s e
3. t h a n k f u l
4. r o m a n t i c
5. e r e c t
6. s e c o n d
7. c h e e r f u l
8. s a f e

Down entries:
- 9: d e f e c t i v (defective)
- 11: e e v e l (level area)
- 13: g r o u c h y
- 15: t o o t h s o m e
- 16: f u n n
- 18: c h u b b y
- 10: r o b u s t
- 12: c l e a n
- 14: c r u e l
- 17: f i r s t
- second column: t h e r e / t

Across
1. Very pleasant
2. Extremely large
3. Happy or grateful because of something
4. Relating to love or a close loving relationship
5. Develop
6. Immediately after the first and before any others
7. Happy and positive
8. Not in danger or likely to be harmed

Down
9. Broken part
10. Strong and unlikely to break or fail
11. At the same height
12. Not dirty
13. Complain in an angry way
14. Causing pain intentionally
15. Attractive or pleasant
16. Not excited
17. Coming before all others
18. Rounded in a pleasant and attractive way

Puzzle #26

```
            6    7
            i  1 t  e  l  l  i  n  g 12
      5     m    o     9            n
   2  m  a  m  m  o  t  h           u
      u     e    t     e            t
      r     n    h  3  a  b  j  e  c t
      k     s    s     d            y
      y     e    o     y
                 m  8     10        11
              4  e  l  a  s  t  i  c
                    e     t         h
                    v     r         u
                    e     a         b
                    l     n         b
                          g         y
                          e
```

Across
1. Revealing
2. Gigantic prehistoric animal
3. Poor, unsuccessful, the state of being extremely unhappy
4. Able to stretch

Down
5. Dark and dirty or difficult to see through
6. Extremely large
7. Attractive or pleasant
8. At the same height
9. Feel slightly drunk
10. Unusual and unexpected
11. Rounded in a pleasant and attractive way
12. Containing, tasting of, or similar to nuts

Puzzle #27

A crossword grid with the following entries:

Across
1. exclusive
2. near
3. nutty
4. erect
5. clean
6. dry
7. discreet

Down
8. normal
9. enthusiasia (enthusias...) — column reads: e n t h u s i a s
10. learned
11. cheerful
12. acidic
13. unarmed
14. inquisitiv (inquisitiv...)
15. round
16. energetic
17. cagey
18. aspiring

Across
1. Limited to only one person
2. Not far away in distance
3. Containing, tasting of, or similar to nuts
4. Develop
5. Not dirty
6. No water or other liquid in
7. Careful not to attract too much attention

Down
8. Ordinary or usual
9. Feeling of energetic interest
10. Showing much knowledge
11. Happy and positive
12. Dissolves materials
13. Not armed
14. Eager to know a lot
15. Shaped like a ball or circle
16. Having a lot of energy
17. Unwilling to give information
18. Someone who is trying to become successful

Puzzle #28

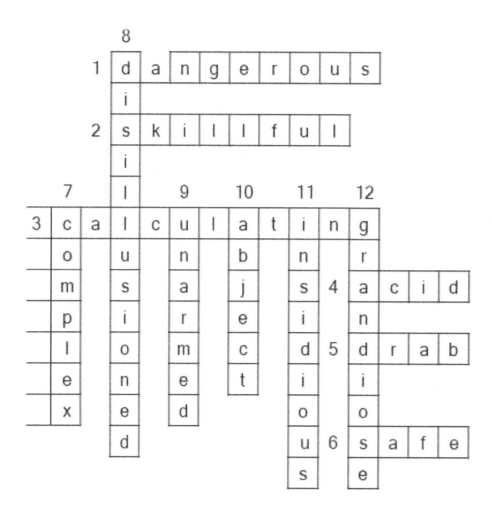

Across
1. Hing, or activity could harm you
2. Ability to do an activity or job well
3. Sing other people or situations as a way to get something you want, esp. in a selfish or secret way
4. Dissolves materials
5. Boring
6. Not in danger or likely to be harmed

Down
7. Difficult to understand
8. Disappointed discovering the truth
9. Not armed
10. Poor, unsuccessful, the state of being extremely unhappy
11. Gradually and secretly causing harm
12. Grand very large

Puzzle #29

		8				10		11		
1	g	u	l	l	i	b	l	e		
		r				a		l		12
6		o		9		d	2	a	c	i	d
3 h	i	d	e	o	u	s					r
a	r	v	4	w	e	a	k		s		a
r	u	y		e				t		b
s	n			e				i		
h	5	k	n	o	t	t	y		c	

Across
1. Easily deceived
2. Dissolves materials
3. Extremely ugly or bad
4. Not physically strong
5. Complicated and difficult to solve

Down
6. Unkind, cruel
7. Drinking too much alcohol
8. Fashionable and interesting
9. Not bitter or salty
10. Unpleasant and causing difficulties or harm, evil, low quality, not acceptable
11. Able to stretch
12. Boring

Puzzle #30

	4	5	6	7			
1	a	m	a	z	i	n	g

Grid:

```
        4   5   6   7
1       a   m   a   z   i   n   g
        n   n   m   2   r   o   u   n   d
        i   x   m       o
        m   i   m       u       8       9
        a   o   e   3   c   l   e   a   n
        t   u   n       h       r       u
        e   s   s       y       e       t
        d       e               c       t
                                t       y
```

Across
1. Extremely surprising, very good, extremely surprised
2. Shaped like a ball or circle
3. Not dirty

Down
4. Excited, interested, enthusiastic
5. Worried, nervous
6. Extremely large
7. Complain in an angry way
8. Develop
9. Containing, tasting of, or similar to nuts

Puzzle #31

```
                    11
                 1 | s | a | d |
                   | w |
        9          | e |        12      13
     2 | c | h | e | e | r | f | u | l |
       | h |   | t |       | o |   | n |
       | u |   |   |       | u |   | i |
     3 | b | i | g |       | n | 4 | n | u | t | t | y |
       | b |   |   |       | d |   | t |        14
       | y |   |   |       |   |   | e | r | e | c | t |
        10                     5 | e |   |   |   | r |
     6 | d | i | s | c | r | e | e | t |   |   | u |
       | r |   |   |   |   |   | s |   |   |   | e |
       | u | 7 | k | n | o | t | t | y |   |   | l |
       | n |   |   |   |   |   | e |
       | k |           8 | d | r | y |
```

Across
1. Unhappy or sorry
2. Happy and positive
3. Large in size or amount
4. Containing, tasting of, or similar to nuts
5. Develop
6. Careful not to attract too much attention
7. Complicated and difficult to solve
8. No water or other liquid in

Down
9. Rounded in a pleasant and attractive way
10. Drinking too much alcohol
11. Not bitter or salty
12. Shaped like a ball or circle
13. Not excited
14. Causing pain intentionally

Puzzle #32

```
                    11
                     s
              1  d  r  a  b
                     i
              2  s  o  l  i  d
                     c
              3  r  o  b  u  s  t
                     e           13
        4  h  o  m  e  l  e  s  s
                     t           w
        8     9    10    12      e
     5  c  o  m  b  a  t  i  v  e
        l     a     b     i      t
        e     t     e     n
        a     u     r     n
        n     r     r     o
              e     r  6  c  r  u  e  l
                    a     e
                    n  7  n  u  t  t  y
                    t     t
```

Across
1. Boring
2. Hard or firm
3. Strong and unlikely to break or fail
4. Without a home
5. Eager to fight or argue
6. Causing pain intentionally
7. Containing, tasting of, or similar to nuts

Down
8. Not dirty
9. Behave like adults
10. Abnormal, deviant, different
11. Careful not to attract too much attention
12. Not guilty of a particular crime
13. Not bitter or salty

Puzzle #33

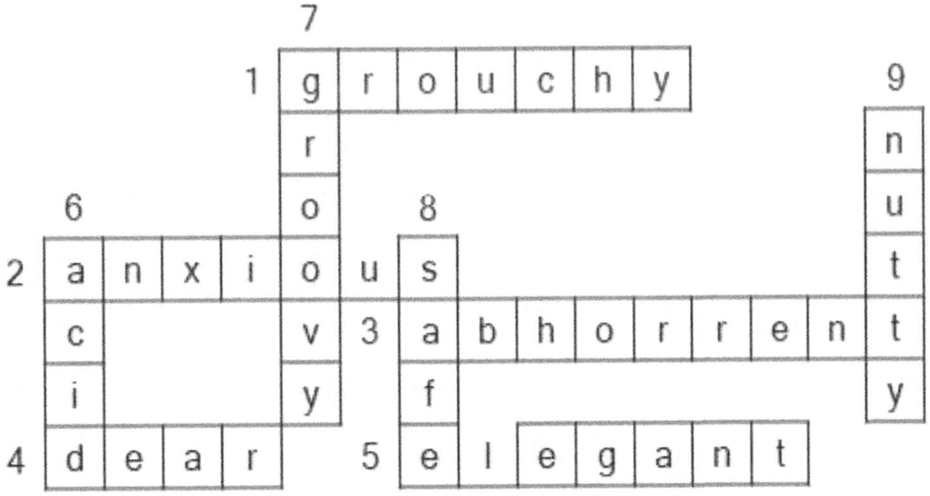
1 grouchy
2 anxious
3 abhorrent
4 dear
5 elegant
6 acid
7 groovy
8 safe
9 nutty

Across

1. Complain in an angry way
2. Worried, nervous
3. Detestable, repugnant, repulsive, morally very bad
4. Loved very much
5. Attractive in appearance

Down

6. Dissolves materials
7. Fashionable and interesting
8. Not in danger or likely to be harmed
9. Containing, tasting of, or similar to nuts

Puzzle #34

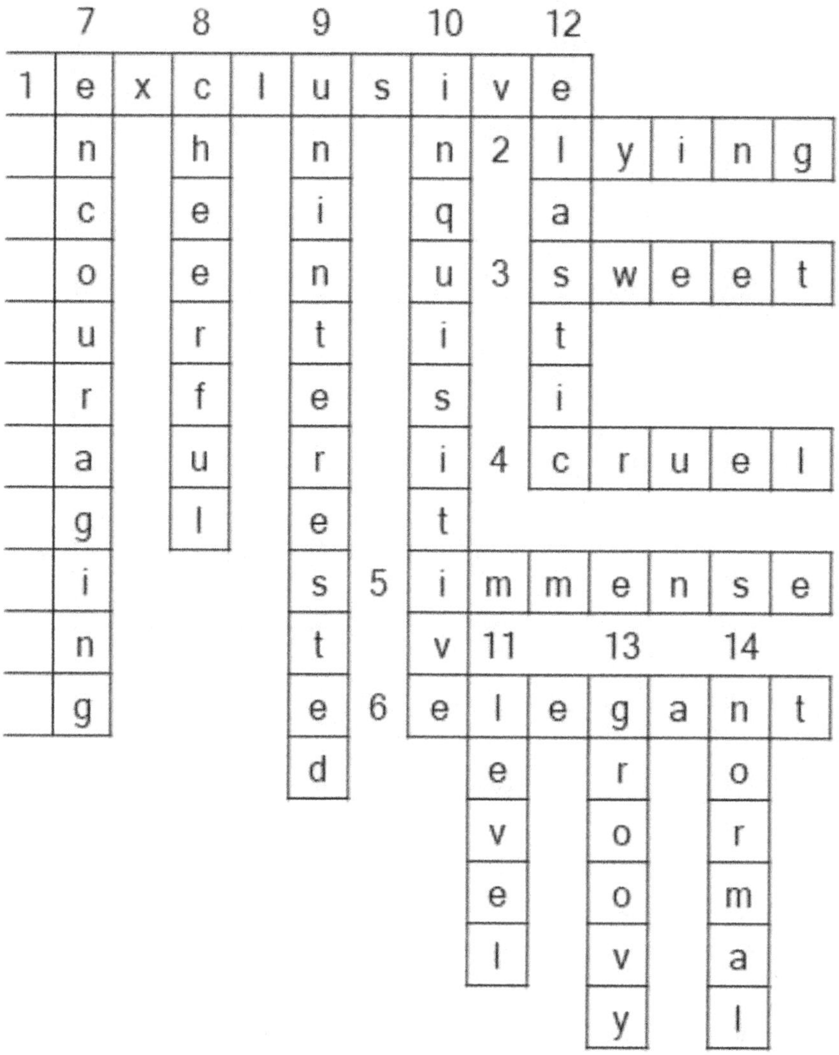

	7	8	9	10	12

Grid (across answers):
- 1. exclusive
- 2. lying
- 3. sweet
- 4. cruel
- 5. immense
- 6. elegant

Down answers:
- 7. encouraging
- 8. cheerful
- 9. cnintierested (uninterested)
- 10. inquisitive
- 12. elastic
- 11. level
- 13. groovy
- 14. normal

Across
1. Limited to only one person
2. Telling not the true
3. Not bitter or salty
4. Causing pain intentionally
5. Extremely large
6. Attractive in appearance

Down
7. Make something more likely to happen
8. Happy and positive
9. Not excited
10. Eager to know a lot
11. At the same height
12. Able to stretch
13. Fashionable and interesting
14. Ordinary or usual

Puzzle #35

```
                                              11
                                              ┌───┐
                                              │ s │
                                              ├───┤
                                              │ w │
                                              ├───┤
                   9                          │ e │
                ┌───┬───┬───┬───┬───┬───┬───┬───┤
              1 │ a │ d │ h │ e │ s │ i │ v │ e │
                ├───┤   └───┘   └───┘       ├───┤
        7     8 │ l │         10            │ t │
    ┌───┬───┬───┼───┼───┬───┐               └───┘
  2 │ s │ k │ i │ l │ l │ f │ u │ l │
    ├───┤   ├───┤   ├───┤   ├───┤            12
    │ e │   │ n │   │ e │   │ n │        ┌───┐
    ├───┤   ├───┤   ├───┼───┬───┬───┬───┬───┤
    │ c │   │ s │   │ g │ 3 │ a │ b │ j │ e │ c │ t │
    ├───┤   ├───┤   ├───┤   ├───┤            │ e │
    │ o │   │ i │   │ e │   │ r │            ├───┤
    ├───┤   ├───┤   ├───┤ 4 │ m │ a │ l │ e │ l │
    │ n │   │ d │   │ d │   ├───┤            ├───┤
    ├───┤   ├───┤   └───┘   │ e │            │ l │
    │ d │   │ i │         5 │ d │ r │ y │    ├───┤
    └───┘   ├───┤           └───┘            │ i │
            │ o │                            ├───┤
            ├───┤                            │ n │
            │ u │                            ├───┤
          6 │ s │ o │ l │ i │ d │            │ g │
            └───┘                            └───┘
```

Across
1. Glue
2. Ability to do an activity or job well
3. Poor, unsuccessful, the state of being extremely unhappy
4. Man
5. No water or other liquid in
6. Hard or firm

Down
7. Immediately after the first and before any others
8. Gradually and secretly causing harm
9. Said or thought by some people to be the stated bad or illegal thing, although you have no proof
10. Not armed
11. Not bitter or salty
12. Revealing

Puzzle #36

A crossword puzzle with the following filled-in answers:

Across:
1. thankful
2. proud
3. energetic
4. internal
5. normal
6. idiotic
7. groovy
8. righteous
9. innocent

Across
1. Happy or grateful because of something
2. Having or showing respect for yourself
3. Having a lot of energy
4. Inside the body
5. Ordinary or usual
6. A foolish idea
7. Fashionable and interesting
8. Morally correct
9. Not guilty of aparticular crime

Down
10. Having a lot of power to control people and events
11. Attractive or pleasant
12. Refusing to obey
13. Relating to love or a close loving relationship
14. Someone who is trying to become successful
15. Causing pain intentionally
16. Telling not the true
17. Not far away in distance
18. Happening or done quickly and without warning

Puzzle #37

1 i	n	s	i	d	i	o	u	s		
m		**10**		**11**		**2** a	m	a	z	i	n	g
3 m	a	t	u	r	e		d			

1 insidious

2 amazing

3 mature

4 flat

5 encouraging

6 idiotic

7 efficacious

8 nutty

Down words visible: immense, smooth, reflect, first, sad, cruel, common, near, second

Across
1. Gradually and secretly causing harm
2. Extremely surprising, very good, extremely surprised
3. Behave like adults
4. Level and smooth
5. Make something more likely to happen
6. A foolish idea
7. Able to produce the intended result
8. Containing, tasting of, or similar to nuts

Down
9. Extremely large
10. Attractive or pleasant
11. Able to send back light a surface
12. Coming before all others
13. Unhappy or sorry
14. Causing pain intentionally
15. Fact that everyone knows
16. Not far away in distance
17. Immediately after the first and before any others

Puzzle #38

		11								
1	s	a	t	i	s	f	y	i	n	g

Grid:
- 1 Across: s a t i s f y i n g
- 11 Down (under t): w e
- 2 Across: a b j e c t
- 9 Down (under a): n x o u
- 13 Down: t l i n g
- 3 Across: e l a s t i c
- 4 Across: i c y
- 5 Across: l e v e l
- 6 Across: n e b u l o u s
- 15 Down: b r o k e n
- 16 Down: u e a r n e d
- 17 Down: s n a r m e d
- 7 Across: s a f e
- 10 Down: s p i r i n g
- 12 Down: e n e r g e t i c
- 14 Down: n u t y
- 8 Across: i n t e r n a l

Across
1. Making you feel pleased by providing what you need or want
2. Poor, unsuccessful, the state of being extremely unhappy
3. Able to stretch
4. Extremely cold
5. At the same height
6. Not clear and having no form
7. Not in danger or likely to be harmed
8. Inside the body

Down
9. Worried, nervous
10. Someone who is trying to become successful
11. Not bitter or salty
12. Having a lot of energy
13. Revealing
14. Containing, tasting of, or similar to nuts
15. Damaged
16. Showing much knowledge
17. Not armed

Puzzle #39

		8		9		10		11		13		
1	e	x	c	l	u	s	i	v	e
	n		a		n		m		l
	e		g		i		m		e
	r		e		n		e		g
7	g		y		t		n		a

Across grid (selected entries):
- 2. s w e e t
- 3. s c a r e d
- 5. n u t t y
- 4. c h e e r f u l
- 6. e l a s t i c

Down entries include: secretive, energgetic, scattic, cagey, uninterested, immmense, elegant, cheerd, flat, scatt

Across
1. Limited to only one person
2. Not bitter or salty
3. Rightened or worried
4. Happy and positive
5. Containing, tasting of, or similar to nuts
6. Able to stretch

Down
7. Not wanting others to know
8. Having a lot of energy
9. Unwilling to give information
10. Not excited
11. Extremely large
12. Level and smooth
13. Attractive in appearance

Puzzle #40

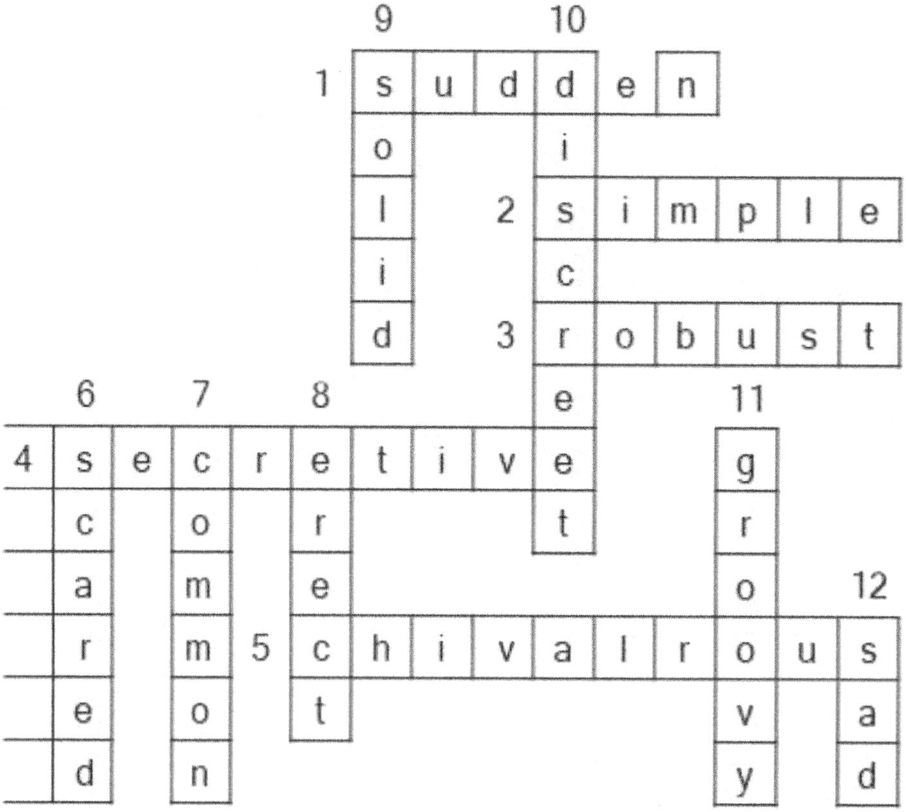
1 sudden
2 simple
3 robust
4 secretive
5 chivalrous
6 scared
7 common
8 erect
9 solid
10 discreet
11 groovy
12 sad

Across

1. Happening or done quickly and without warning
2. Not difficult
3. Strong and unlikely to break or fail
4. Not wanting others to know
5. Polite, honest, fair, and kind

Down

6. Rightened or worried
7. Fact that everyone knows
8. Develop
9. Hard or firm
10. Careful not to attract too much attention
11. Fashionable and interesting
12. Unhappy or sorry

Puzzle #41

		12		14						
1	g	r	o	o	v	y				
	r		u							
	a	2	t	o	o	t	h	s	o	m	e
	t		r							
	e	3	a	b	e	r	r	a	n	t
	f		g							
	u	4	e	l	a	s	t	i	c	
	l		o							

Across

1. Fashionable and interesting
2. Attractive or pleasant
3. Abnormal, deviant, different
4. Able to stretch
5. Not armed
6. Without a home
7. Unpleasant and causing difficulties or unusual harm, evil, low quality, not acceptable
8. Said or thought by some people to be the stated bad or illegal thing, although you have no proof

Down

9. Unkind, cruel
10. Fact that everyone knows
11. At the same height
12. Expressing thanks
13. Unhappy or sorry
14. Unacceptable, offensive, violent, or unusual
15. Dissolves materials
16. Nothing more than
17. Boring
18. Happening or done quickly and without warning

Grid answers:
- 1 Across: groovy
- 2 Across: toothsome
- 3 Across: aberrant
- 4 Across: elastic
- 6 Across: homeless
- 7 Across: bad
- 8 Across: alleged
- 5 Down (unarmed): unarmed
- 6 Down: harsh
- 9 Down: harsh
- 10 Down: common
- 11 Down: leveled
- 12 Down: grateful
- 13 Down: unarmed / sad
- 14 Down: outrageous
- 15 Down: acidic
- 16 Down: merere
- 17 Down: drab
- 18 Down: sudden

Puzzle #42

		9		10				11	1	12	a	b	o	a	r	d

2 h o m e l e s s
a a n 3 p l a i n
l j t i
t e h 4 r o u n d
i s u i 14
n t s 5 n u t t y
g i i g h
c a 6 a c i d
s 13 n
t s k
i w 7 f l a t
c e u 15
8 t e l l i n g
t o
d
l
y

Across
1. On or onto a ship, aircraft, bus, or train
2. Without a home
3. Not decorated in any way; with nothing added
4. Shaped like a ball or circle
5. Containing, tasting of, or similar to nuts
6. Dissolves materials
7. Level and smooth
8. Revealing

Down
9. Stopping and starting repeatedly
10. Beautiful, powerful, or causing great admiration and respect
11. Feeling of energetic interest
12. Someone who is trying to become successful
13. Not bitter or salty
14. Happy or grateful because of something
15. Respecting God

Puzzle #43

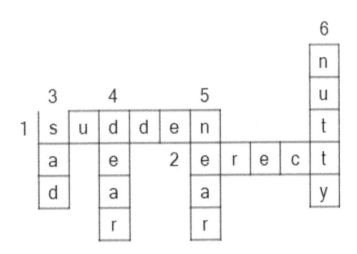

Across

1. Happening or done quickly and without warning
2. Develop

Down

3. Unhappy or sorry
4. Loved very much
5. Not far away in distance
6. Containing, tasting of, or similar to nuts

Puzzle #44

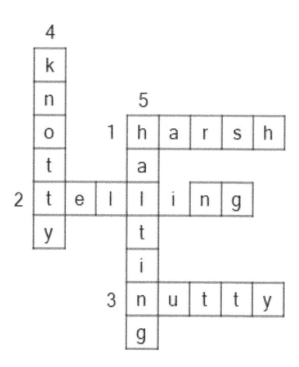

Across
1. Unkind, cruel
2. Revealing
3. Containing, tasting of, or similar to nuts

Down
4. Complicated and difficult to solve
5. Stopping and starting repeatedly

Puzzle #45

```
                    11                                 13
                 1  a  d  h  e  s  i  v  e
                    b                      r
              2  c  h  e  e  r  f  u  l     e
              9        10       r        12 c
           3  p  o  w  e  r  f  u  l        t
              l        h     a     n
              a        o     n  4  i  d  i  o  t  i  c
              i        l     t     n
              n        e        5  t  h  a  n  k  f  u  l
                                   e
                                6  r  o  m  a  n  t  i  c  14
                                   e                       s
                                7  s  a  d                 w
                                   t                       e
                                8  e  x  c  l  u  s  i  v  e
                                   d                       t
```

Across
1. Glue
2. Happy and positive
3. Having a lot of power to control people and events
4. A foolish idea
5. Happy or grateful because of something
6. Relating to love or a close loving relationship
7. Unhappy or sorry
8. Limited to only one person

Down
9. Not decorated in any way; with nothing added
10. Complete or not divided
11. Abnormal, deviant, different
12. Not excited
13. Develop
14. Not bitter or salty

Puzzle #46

```
        3       4       5       6
1   i   n   n   o   c   e   n   t
    d       e       l       u
    i       b       e       t
    o       u       a       t
    t       l       n       y
    i       o
    c       u
2           s   i   m   p   l   e
```

Across
1. Not guilty of a particular crime
2. Not difficult

Down
3. A foolish idea
4. Not clear and having no form
5. Not dirty
6. Containing, tasting of, or similar to nuts

Puzzle #47

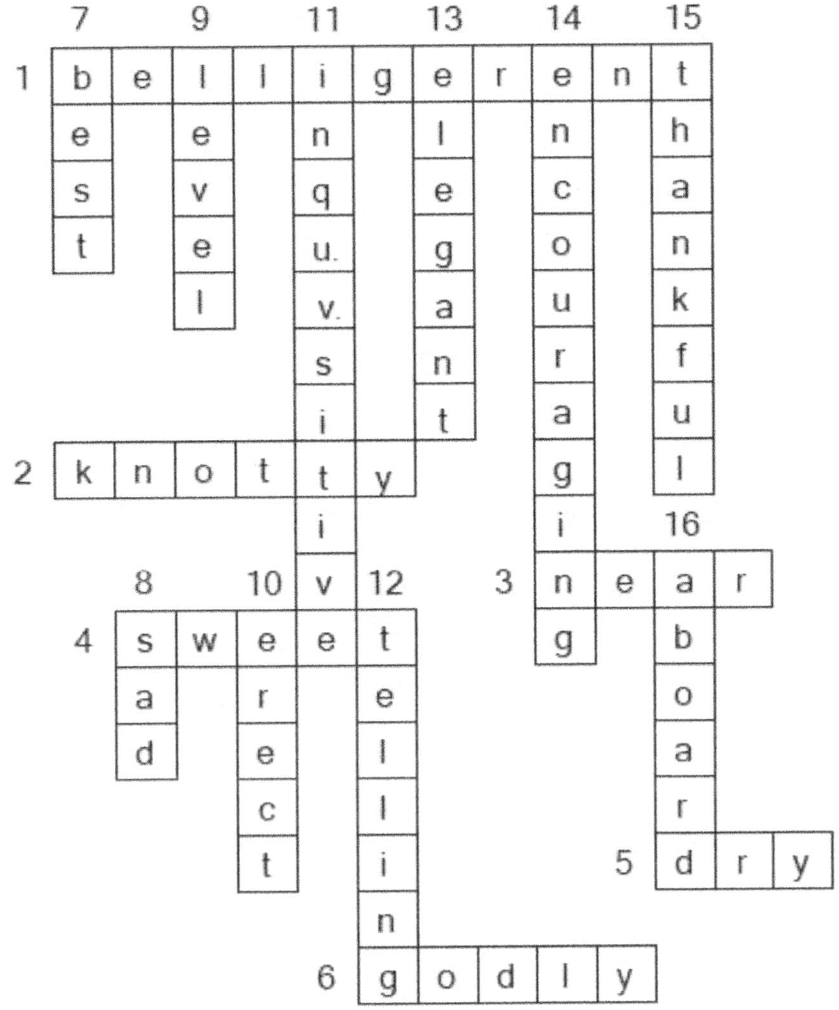

1 belligerent
2 knotty
3 near
4 sweet
5 dry
6 godly
7 best
8 sad
9 level
10 erect
11 inquisitiv
12 telling
13 elegant
14 encouraging
15 thankful
16 aboard

Across

1. Disapproving, wishing to fight or argue
2. Complicated and difficult to solve
3. Not far away in distance
4. Not bitter or salty
5. No water or other liquid in
6. Respecting God

Down

7. Most excellent, highest quality,
8. Unhappy or sorry
9. At the same height
10. Develop
11. Eager to know a lot
12. Revealing
13. Attractive in appearance
14. Make something more likely to happen
15. Happy or grateful because of something
16. On or onto a ship, aircraft, bus, or train

Puzzle #48

Across
1. Unkind, cruel
2. Gigantic prehistoric animal
3. At the same height
4. Hard or firm
5. Unacceptable, offensive, violent, or unusual
6. Stupid, unreasonable, silly in a humorous way, things that happen that are unreasonable
7. Nothing more than
8. Unhappy or sorry
9. No water or other liquid in

Down
10. Fashionable and interesting
11. Complicated and difficult to solve
12. Worried, nervous
13. Happy and positive
14. Not armed
15. Without a home
16. Boring

Puzzle #49

		12									

Crossword grid:

1 Across: s a f e
12 Down: s w e e t
2 Across: b r o w n
3 Across: e l e g a n t
14 Down: t e l l i n g
7 Down: b u r l y
8 Down: o u t r a g e o u s
9 Down: n e b u l o u s
4 Across: a l l e g e d
13 Down: d r a b
5 Across: s t r a n g e
10 Down: r o b u s t
11 Down: n u t t y
6 Across: k n o t t y

Across
1. Not in danger or likely to be harmed
2. The color of chocolate
3. Attractive in appearance
4. Said or thought by some people to be the stated bad or illegal thing, although you have no proof
5. Unusual and unexpected
6. Complicated and difficult to solve

Down
7. Large and strong
8. Unacceptable, offensive, violent, or unusual
9. Not clear and having no form
10. Strong and unlikely to break or fail
11. Containing, tasting of, or similar to nuts
12. Not bitter or salty
13. Boring
14. Revealing

Puzzle #50

Across
1. Containing, tasting of, or similar to nuts
2. Eager to know a lot
3. Telling not the true
4. Boring
5. Respecting God
6. Not far away in distance
7. No water or other liquid in

Down
8. Not guilty of a particular crime
9. Not armed
10. Happening or done quickly and without warning
11. Develop
12. Complicated and difficult to solve
13. Shaped like a ball or circle
14. Attractive in appearance
15. Refusing to obey

Puzzle #51

```
        8       9       11
   1  p   l   a   i   n
      a   r   2  e   r   e   c   t
      l   o       a                           16
      e   m   3  r   i   g   h   t   e   o   u   s
          a                                    a
   4  t   e   l   l   i   n   g          5  d   r   y
      i   10      12      13      14      15
   6  c   a   l   c   u   l   a   t   i   n   g
          n       l       e       h       u
          x       e       a       a       t
          i       a       r       n       t
          o       n       n       k       y
          u               e       f
          s               d       u
                              7  l   y   i   n   g
```

Across
1. Not decorated in any way; with nothing added
2. Develop
3. Morally correct
4. Revealing
5. No water or other liquid in
6. Sing other people or situations as a way to get something you want, esp. in a selfish or secret way
7. Telling not the true

Down
8. Having less color than usual
9. Having a pleasant smell
10. Worried, nervous
11. Not far away in distance
12. Not dirty
13. Showing much knowledge
14. Happy or grateful because of something
15. Containing, tasting of, or similar to nuts
16. Unhappy or sorry

Puzzle #52

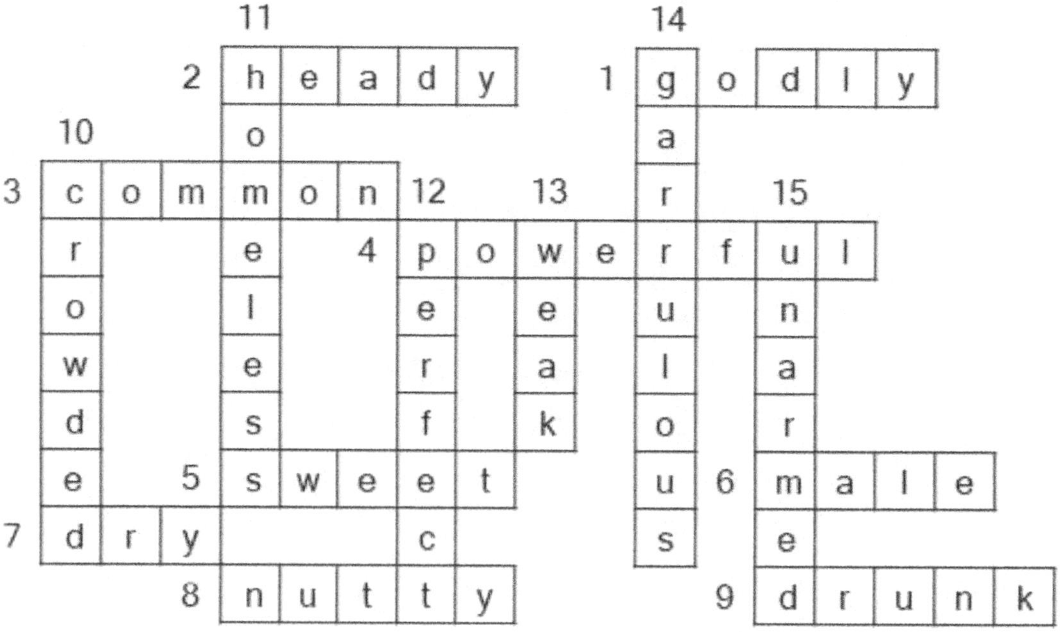

2 heady
1 godly
3 common
4 powerful
5 sweet
6 male
7 dry
8 nutty
9 drunk
10 crowded
11 homeless
12 perfect
13 weak
14 garrulous
15 unarmed

Across

1. Respecting God
2. Feel slightly drunk
3. Fact that everyone knows
4. Having a lot of power to control people and events
5. Not bitter or salty
6. Man
7. No water or other liquid in
8. Containing, tasting of, or similar to nuts
9. Drinking too much alcohol

Down

10. Full of people
11. Without a home
12. Complete and correct in every way, of the best possible type or without fault
13. Not physically strong
14. Habit of talking a lot
15. Not armed

Puzzle #53

	5	6	7	8	10		
1	h	i	l	a	r	i	o	u	s

Crossword grid:

- Across 1: h i l a r i o u s
- Down 5: h a r s h
- Down 6: i l e v e l
- Down 7: l o m a n t i c
- Down 8: a u t r a g e o u s
- Down 10: r a
- Across 2: d r y
- Down 12: y r o b u s t
- Across 3: s w e e t
- Down 9: w h o l e
- Down 11: e l e g a n t
- Across 4: k n o t t y

Across
1. Extremely funny
2. No water or other liquid in
3. Not bitter or salty
4. Complicated and difficult to solve

Down
5. Unkind, cruel
6. At the same height
7. Relating to love or a close loving relationship
8. Unacceptable, offensive, violent, or unusual
9. Complete or not divided
10. Unhappy or sorry
11. Attractive in appearance
12. Strong and unlikely to break or fail

Puzzle #54

A crossword puzzle grid with the following answers:

Across
1. skillful
2. anxious
3. mammoth
4. drunk
5. cheerful
6. safe
7. enthusiastic

Down
8. combative
9. exclusive
10. secretive
11. robust
12. immense
13. learned
14. lying
15. unarmed
16. righteous
17. normal
18. halting

1. Ability to do an activity or job well
2. Worried, nervous
3. Gigantic prehistoric animal
4. Drinking too much alcohol
5. Happy and positive
6. Not in danger or likely to be harmed
7. Feeling of energetic interest

Down
8. Eager to fight or argue
9. Limited to only one person
10. Not wanting others to know
11. Strong and unlikely to break or fail
12. Extremely large
13. Showing much knowledge
14. Telling not the true
15. Not armed
16. Morally correct
17. Ordinary or usual
18. Stopping and starting repeatedly

Puzzle #55

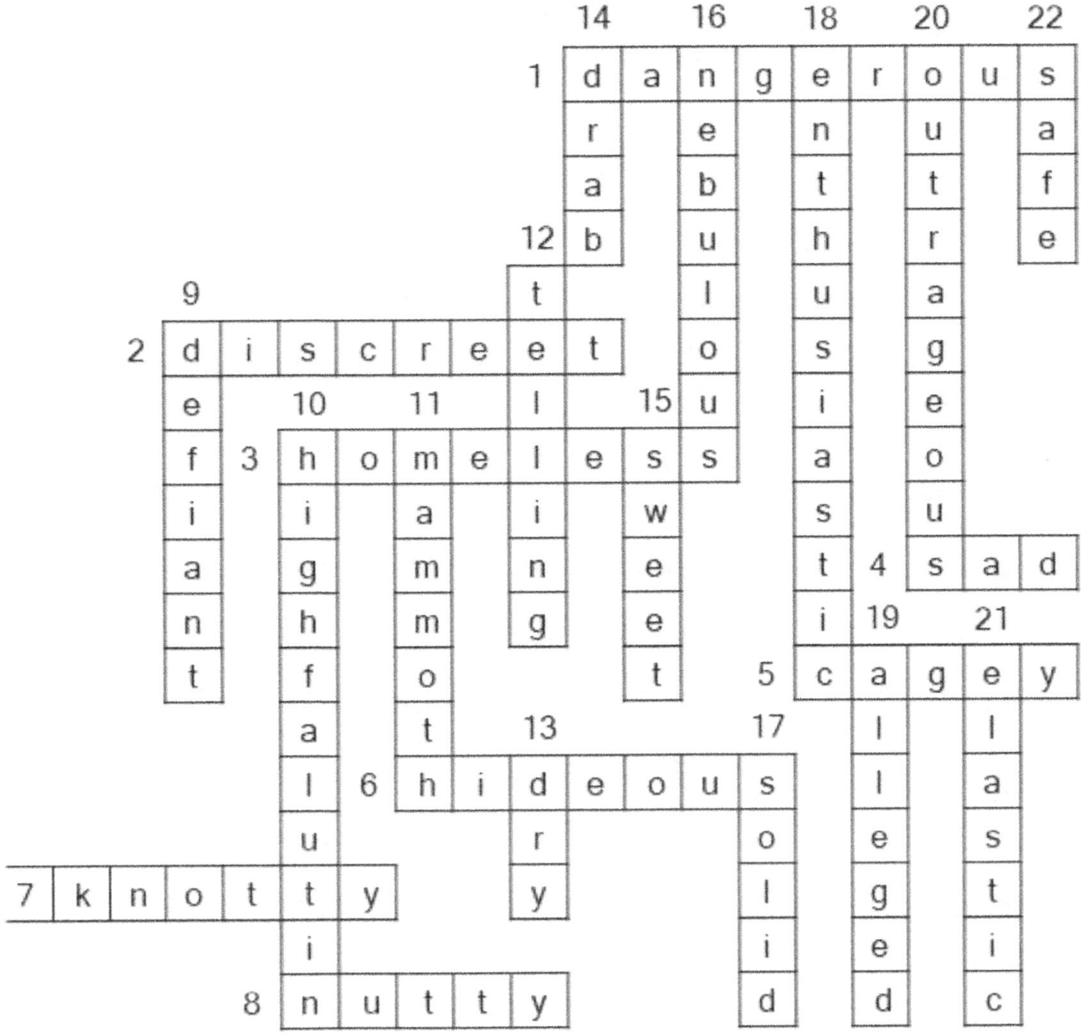

A crossword puzzle grid with the following filled-in answers:

Across:
1. dangerous
2. discreet
3. homeless
4. sad
5. cagey
6. hideous
7. knotty
8. nutty

Down:
9. defiant
10. highfalutin
11. mammoth
12. but
13. dry
14. drab
15. sweet
16. nebulous
17. solid
18. enthusiastic
19. alleged
20. outrageous
21. elastic
22. safe

Across
1. Hing, or activity could harm you
2. Careful not to attract too much attention
3. Without a home
4. Unhappy or sorry
5. Unwilling to give information
6. Extremely ugly or bad
7. Complicated and difficult to solve
8. Containing, tasting of, or similar to nuts

Down
9. Refusing to obey
10. Trying to seem very important
11. Gigantic prehistoric animal
12. Revealing
13. No water or other liquid in
14. Boring
15. Not bitter or salty
16. Not clear and having no form
17. Hard or firm
18. Feeling of energetic interest
19. Said or thought by some people to be the stated bad or illegal thing, although you have no proof
20. Unacceptable, offensive, violent, or unusual
21. Able to stretch
22. Not in danger or likely to be harmed

Puzzle #56

		3			4				
1	s	u	d	d	e	n			

Across
1. Happening or done quickly and without warning
2. Coming before all others

Down
3. Not difficult
4. Not the same
5. Strong and unlikely to break or fail
6. Revealing

Puzzle #56

```
        3           4
    1 │ s │ u │ d │ d │ e │ n │
      │ i │       │ i │
      │ m │       │ f │       5       6
      │ p │   2 │ f │ i │ r │ s │ t │
      │ l │       │ e │   │ o │   │ e │
      │ e │       │ r │   │ b │   │ l │
              │ e │   │ u │   │ l │
              │ n │   │ s │   │ i │
              │ t │   │ t │   │ n │
                              │ g │
```

Across
1. Happening or done quickly and without warning
2. Coming before all others

Down
3. Not difficult
4. Not the same
5. Strong and unlikely to break or fail
6. Revealing

Puzzle #57

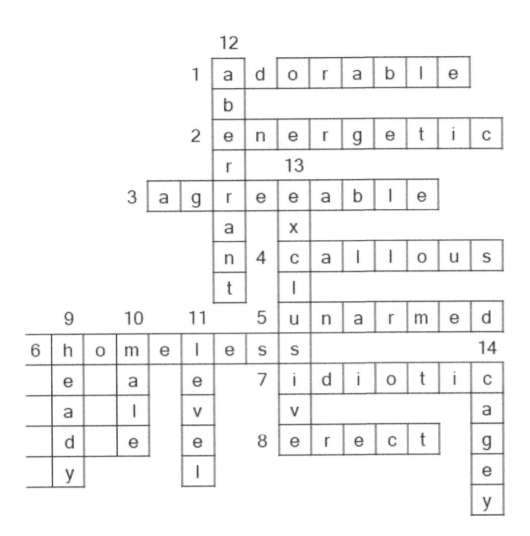

Across
1. Attractive, appealing, lovely, charming, and easily loved
2. Having a lot of energy
3. Accepted, accept something
4. Unkind, cruel, without sympathy
5. Not armed
6. Without a home
7. A foolish idea
8. Develop

Down
9. Feel slightly drunk
10. Man
11. At the same height
12. Abnormal, deviant, different
13. Limited to only one person
14. Unwilling to give information

Puzzle #58

Across
1. No water or other liquid in
2. Excited, interested, enthusiastic
3. Revealing
4. Not armed
5. A foolish idea
6. Rounded in a pleasant and attractive way
7. Ability to do an activity or job well
8. Careful not to attract too much attention
9. Not guilty of a particular crime
10. Level and smooth

Down
11. Happening or done quickly and without warning
12. Not in danger or likely to be harmed
13. Boring
14. Impossible to defeat
15. Worried, nervous
16. Feeling of energetic interest

Made in United States
North Haven, CT
22 May 2022

19427298R00070